fabrics

By Caroline Lebeau

Photographs by Jacques Dirand

Text by Patricia Corbett

THAMES AND HUDSON

fabrics

THE DECORATIVE ART OF TEXTILES

To Yveline, Caroline, Joseph, and Adrien
To Martin, Marco, Claire, Marc, Paola, and Adrien

First published in Great Britain in 1994
by Thames and Hudson Ltd, London, by
arrangement with Clarkson N. Potter, Inc.,
201 East 50th Street, New York, NY 10022.

British Library Cataloguing-in-Publication Data

A catalogue record for this book is available from the British
Library

ISBN 0-500-01631-3

Printed and bound in Japan

HALF-TITLE PAGE: *Detail of a silk taffeta bedcover
and hangings in Jacques Garcia's house in Paris.*

TITLE PAGE: *A silver brocade border for Napoleon
Bonaparte's bedroom in the Grand Trianon.*

ABOVE: *Fashion designer Chantal Thomass adds
heart-shaped cushions to René Prou chairs.*

contents

LEFT: *A printed cotton sample from the Koechlin Ziegler factory in Mulhouse, roller-printed between 1827 and 1840. Motifs representing lace, feathers, and cherubs were often specially printed for the Spanish market.* ABOVE: La Toile de Penelope, *an early-eighteenth-century engraving by B. Picart, shows the faithful wife at her loom.*

It took Penelope's unwelcome suitors over three years to realize that Ulysses' loyal wife had duped them, weaving her great web by day, then secretly unraveling it after dusk by torchlight—to stall the hour when she might have to choose a new husband from among their number. Even so, the suitors did not detect her ruse themselves; they were tipped off by one of the queen's attendants.

Few laymen actually understand the process of weaving, yet in all eras and latitudes cloth remains a constant in the human environment: a guarantee of physical comfort and protection, a symbol of power, or a mark of honor, depending on the circumstances. Loincloths and lingerie, brollies and yurts, red carpets, white flags, and mosquito netting may be utter necessities—or emphatic visual statements. Our most vividly recalled episodes from the Old and New Testaments feature swaddling bands, Joseph's coat of many colors, Veronica's veil, or Christ's seamless robes; the Shroud of Turin is still venerated by many as Catholicism's holiest relic. Scary tales such as "Rumpelstiltskin" and "Sleeping Beauty," where near-death and destruction are only a pinprick away, have enthralled generations. We speak of silver linings, but know with Shake-

introduction

speare that "the web of life is a mingled yarn, good and ill together."

Spinning and weaving were accomplishments worthy of Olympus. Life hung by a thread in the hands of the three Fates, daughters of Night. Persephone created an image of the universe on her loom in the grotto of Cyane; Apollo, worshiped as the author of the grid pattern typical of Greek settlements, was called the Weaver of Cities; and Athena transformed her mortal rival, Arachne, into a spider because she dared surpass the goddess in a weaving contest. (To this day, it is still customary for ethnic weavers in some parts of the world to include a small, deliberate error in their work as proof of the imperfection of human manufacture, to propitiate the deities.)

The spindle and loom are prominently featured in mythologies and religions on the five continents, not as the humble household tools they became in most civilizations, but as instruments of creation. In Taoism, the to-and-fro of the shuttle echoes the rise and fall of breathing; Indians liken the warp to the world, and the weft to the progression of time; to some

....

ABOVE: *Minerva, the Roman goddess of war, transforms her mortal rival, Arachne, into a spider, in one of a series of engravings by Giovanni Mattei for* Les Métamorphoses d'Ovide *by N. Renouard, Paris, 1651.*
LEFT: *"Kalmuk Women in their Tent," a nineteenth-century illustration depicting the nomadic use of fabric among this Mongolian people.*

African tribes, the warp beam represents heaven, and the cloth beam, earth; for Islam, the loom embodies the very structure of the cosmos. Weaving was a religious duty for the Great Lakes Arapaho nation. In Ceylon and Indonesia, textile workers study astrology, divination, and magic.

In most cultures the twining and meshing of threads, which evoke the concepts of marriage, fertility, and childbirth, are considered singularly female occupations; Maori women today undergo purification rites before being initiated into their craft. Though politically incorrect, weavers' terms such as "spinster" or "distaff" are still applied to women in Western culture. Textile working has become a popular icon, of industry in general and female virtue in particular. Conversely, the unmanning of Hercules is exemplified by the hero's bondage to the Lydian queen Omphale, at whose feet he lolled spinning. And less-than-subtle erotic innuendo often tinges Renaissance and Baroque images of women voluptuously turning upright spindles between their palms.

There were and are exceptions. In ancient Egypt, according to Herodotus, linen was the product of male industry, as cotton still is in Mali and Sudan. And in the traditional Hispanic cultures of the Southwestern United States, weaving was a man's prerogative.

The origin of textiles—exactly when and why our ancestors began to use interlaced plant and animal fiber instead of pelts for clothing and shelter—remains a mystery. The plaited effect of crossed palm branches, the spider's web, and the bird's nest have all been suggested as sources for man's earliest matting; Freud even suggested that body hair might have inspired prehistoric garb.

Archeological digs in very dry or very humid

LEFT: *A portrait of the "Célèbre Ylandera" twisting flax fibers before rolling them onto a spindle hangs in the National Flax Museum in Flanders, Belgium.*
RIGHT: *A plaited palm from the West Indies and the nest of a North African weaverbird—probable inspirations for the first woven textiles.*

climates (Egypt, South America, northern steppes and bogs), in which textiles are best preserved, have unearthed spun and meshed fibrous material. These artifacts are so crudely fashioned that they appear almost indistinguishable from basketry. The oldest European finds, uncovered under several meters of silt off the Danish coastline at Ertebolle, date to the late Mesolithic Age, about 4600–3200 B.C. The scraps excavated at Guitarrero, high in the Peruvian Sierra del Norte, are at least twice as ancient. Needles, carding combs, and spindles litter the floors of Stone Age dwellings. And on sites from Syria to Japan, where no woven specimens have survived, earthenware carries irrefutable secondary evidence: pots are impressed with the netlike patterns of the textiles on which they were set to dry.

The Materials

Animal, vegetable, and mineral were, until the twentieth century, the main categories of cloth. Around the world, the fur of mammals—ranging from the Mexican wild rabbit to the Himalayan yak—is used to create woolen yarns. The hairs are obtained by shearing once or twice a year, or—in some nomadic cultures— collected from branches against which the animals have rubbed. The sturdiest and warmest of all fibers, with great variety of texture and color, wool is also naturally fire retardant and dye absorbent. Its worth, even in the ancient world, is graphically illustrated by the myth of the Golden Fleece, sought by Jason and his fifty Argonauts.

Some believe the Fleece to be a metaphor for the most precious of all fibers, silk. Because of the secrecy surrounding its production in China, where it probably originated during the third millennium B.C., Occidentals believed it was a plant derivative. Actually silk is obtained by boiling and unwinding silkworm casings, then reeling out the filaments. Sericulture has always been a lengthy and expensive business. Processing the cocoons is only the last step in

LEFT: *An early-nineteenth-century chromolith from Hungary illustrates the various species of silkworms and butterflies. Two engravings after Jean Stradan, ca. 1600, depicting sericulture—the gathering of mulberry leaves,* TOP, *and women at work sorting, processing, and unwinding the cocoons,* ABOVE.

FOLLOWING PAGES: *Samples of the different stages of linen production, from flax bundle with seed bolls, far left, to skeins of thread, top right.*

the saga. First, there are mulberry orchards to be tended, since the *Bombyx mori* feeds exclusively on the leaves of this tree. Supple and lustrous, silk thread, which may measure up to 1.5 kilometers in length, is easily woven.

Marine silk, or sea wool, is neither silk nor wool, but the byssus, or "beard," of the squamous bivalve mollusk. The Arab weavers of antiquity transformed its yard-long strands into a marvelous, iridescent cloth that shifted hues according to the light—a remote precursor of today's thermosensitive synthetics.

Almost every plant on earth can be used for its fiber: banana, nettle, yucca, China grass, and even coconut husks. Flax is the most highly

prized of the bast (inner bark) fibers, as well as one of the most labor intensive: it must be retted, broken, scutched, hackled, and bleached before being spun to produce linen. Despite the fact that it creases more readily than any other commonly used fabric, linen is supremely elegant and ages well, resisting both soil and pests. Jute, used mostly for sacking, is the poor man's linen, because of its musty odor and tendency to yellow. The leaves of the African raffia palm are dried to a sandy shade, then combed and woven to form jaunty trim, or floor and wall coverings.

Cotton is king, and especially so in the Southern Hemisphere. The fibers come from the boll, a downy white casing for the seeds, which must be removed by ginning. The cotton plant grows best in a climate with heavy rainfall during germination. A dry season at the time the bolls mature guarantees low-breakage thread. From the Indus Valley, where it was bartered as early as the second millennium B.C., cotton spread to Africa: a thirteenth-century Italian explorer wondered at the "wool" that grew there on trees. In the New World, cotton became a symbol of the South before the Civil War and today remains a prime crop. Sea Island is the highest grade of cotton, with long, fine filaments, followed by the Egyptian, American, and Indian varieties.

The magic of mineral fibers is not only universal but immemorial; their special properties, great beauty, or price marked them as status symbols. Fireproof garments of asbestos were known in antiquity; the secret of their fabrication was preserved through the Middle Ages. Silver and gold threads are common to all eras and cultures, from Lapland (where craftsmen flatten the strands by drawing them through their teeth) to China (where metal is hammered onto rice paper, then cut into thin strips). By the thirteenth century, a more flexible thread, called gimp, was obtained by wrapping the metal strands around a silken core.

An intricate silk weave with a gold-leaf design.

LEFT: *A view of the cotton spinning mill at Roubaix.* CLOCKWISE FROM BELOW: *The great weaving atelier at Roubaix. An engraving of a blind worker at his loom by J. Ribault, 1817. A cotton jacquard coverlet is draped over a chair in the Green Chamber of the Von Echstedt manor, near Karlstad, Sweden. A jacquard loom in a Lyons silk factory, ca. 1830. "Mechanized Spinning," from a school manual on industry, ca. 1860.*
BELOW RIGHT: *A looped and cut velvet bow motif on a silk façonné background.*

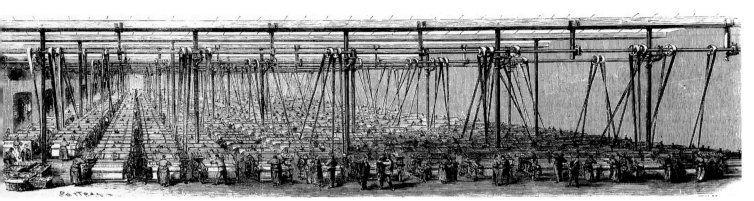

Cloth of gold often provided an accurate measure of royal prestige. In 1476, Charles the Bold, Duke of Burgundy, fled the Swiss troops at Grandson, leaving a battlefield impressively littered with 160 gold cloths, in addition to 400 silk tents. And almost fifty years later, François I splurged 38,505 livres and 10 sols for cloths of gold and silver, as an appropriately grand backdrop for his encounter with Henry VIII in what was thereafter dubbed the Field of Cloth of Gold. Many such textiles have not survived: in times of penury, they were burned to recover their metal content. Louis XVI thus sacrificed a rich brocade that had been commissioned by Louis XV.

Modern fabric discoveries fall into two categories, artificial and synthetic—both virtually indestructible, though not invariably attractive. Artificial fibers, derived from organic substances such as wood cellulose, casein, or peanut and soybean protein, were discovered in the 1880s. Fibranne, rayon, and viscose are the best-known materials in this group. The family of synthetics, derived more recently from petrochemical products, includes acrylics (Dralon, Orlon), polyamides (nylon), and polyesters (Tergal, Dacron, Trevira). Though less glamorous than cloth of gold, both artificial and synthetic filaments require only minimal maintenance, and can be combined with natural yarns for remarkable strength or novel textures.

Techniques and Machines

The implements and the graceful, monotonous gestures used in weaving have survived practically unchanged since their invention. All animal and plant fibers except silk must be spun in order to form a continuous, sturdy yarn from short-staple, sometimes fragile filaments. This is done most simply by twisting the fibers together between index finger and thumb, before they are rolled onto a spindle, which may be dead (fixed) or alive (rotating). The spinning wheel driven by a pedal was introduced during the fifteenth century; around that time, Leonardo da Vinci drew up a project for a mechanized wheel that was never realized. The real breakthrough came with Britain's Industrial Revolution in the second half of the eighteenth century, when Richard Arkwright, John Kendrow, and Thomas Porthow discovered how to power their automatic spinning engines with steam. After the invention of the cotton gin in 1793 by Eli Whitney, textile production on both sides of the Atlantic moved out of the

PRECEDING PAGES: *Cut velvet swirls on a silk madras check background.*

....

RIGHT: *The vibrant colors of vegetable-dyed textiles from the Huehuetenango and Totonicapán departments of Guatemala. Two illustrations from the* Encyclopédie Diderot et D'Alembert *on the art of textiles depict the various operations involved in the dyeing of silk,* TOP, *and the drying process, whereby silk is suspended over a shaking mechanism,* ABOVE.

....

home and small atelier and into the factories.

After spinning, weaving may begin. It is not coincidental that the word "heirloom" stands for some precious or useful item, handed down from generation to generation: in many contemporary rural or nomadic cultures, the loom represents a family's steadiest source of income, the last stage of a domestic production line for household goods. The framework of the loom is uncomplicated, whether the portable back-strap (or body tension) apparatus of the Andean highlands, or the mammoth, onomatopoeic *bistanclaque* still clattering away in a few Lyons silk ateliers. Vertical warp threads are drawn taut within a frame fitted with weights or wheels to maintain tension. The weft is inter-

laced by means of a shuttle traveling back and forth horizontally between alternate rows of warps. In order to facilitate the shuttle's passage, the warps are separated by means of a shed stick, batten, or heddles.

Double, treble, or multiple heddle draw-looms brought greater precision and rapidity to weaving, especially when they were conveniently operated by treadle. Button looms introduced the convenience of easily manipulated hand-pulls regulating the weft. The greatest advance, however, was the Jacquard loom, introduced in 1800, with perforated cards (much like player-piano rolls) that allow weavers to program fabric designs and to dispense with the drawboy's assistance. The ultimate feat will be the "direct Jacquard," a so far hypothetical procedure capable of controlling the entire process, from design to weaving, via floppy disk.

Weaves

There are three basic binding systems—tabby, twill, and satin—but their variations are innumerable, and applicable to all fibers. For collectors, the fascination of textiles is in the variety of weaves; to fabric designers, the same variety presents an almost inexhaustible creative challenge. The most elementary is the tabby weave, in which warp and weft cross each at right angles; it is used for poplin, taffeta, and tweed. Tabbies may also have looped warps or wefts. A simple looped fabric is terrycloth. When the loops are cut, plush, velvet, or corduroy is the result. Twills, including denim, are characterized by diagonals; when the direction of the weft is continuously reversed, a herringbone effect is achieved. Satins may be either weft- or warp-faced, with long, closely set passes of either thread used to create satin's distinctive smooth, compact surface.

Unpatterned fabrics are made on simple cam looms; a dobby attachment is used to produce small geometric designs. Compound weaves, however, in which several weave structures are combined, require the fine-tuning of the Jac-

quard. Damask is a reversible fabric of one or two colors in which figures are defined by the contrast of weft- and warp-faced satin. Brocatelle is a weave with two warps, resulting in slightly raised designs, mostly in satin against a plain ground. In lampas, supplementary wefts and warps are used to add colors to the face of the fabric, then tucked into the back. The nuances of brocade are achieved by spooling extra threads throughout the weave to raise the surface of the design.

Tinting, Printing, and Finishing

Color may indeed have been the luxury of the poor, but today even the rich cannot buy the chromatic exuberance that once made the choice of a bolt of cloth—for a gown, upholstery, a set of bed hangings—a powerful expression of individuality. Before her marriages, Lucrezia Borgia monopolized the ateliers of Rome, Florence, and Venice. On a more modest scale, Louis XIV's morganatic wife, Madame de Maintenon, reminisced about fashioning with her own hands the borders for her yellow damask curtains ("enough to cover ten houses . . . and to turn the stomachs of the Chinese") in the days when she was merely Madame Scarron, wife of the poet Paul. The brilliance, intensity, and subtle variation in hue have been drained by the standardization not only of dyeing, but also of spinning and weaving. Today the goal is a uniform, not a handcrafted, product.

Before the Conquest, Peruvian weavers knew how to produce a staggering 190 shades using combinations of vegetable extracts. The Chinese have at least nineteen words for silk, from *gao* (white silk) to *qi* (patterned silk) to *qian* (blue-red silk). The pinnacle of European inventiveness came during the Baroque era, when the use of "drugs" from the Orient and the Americas—saffron, indigo, quercitron,

brazilwood, among others—was perfected to produce a rainbow of tints. Connoisseurs invented titles still in use today: parakeet green, lobster, pearl gray, peachblossom. There were twelve categories of blue to be had in Lucca, along with the famous Italian *"color d'aria."* Green could be emerald, carnation, duck, or moss. Description-defying terms such as "chimney scrapings," "mortal sin," and "dying monkey" were concocted, as well as other, less abstruse epithets: *"cheveux de la reine"* (in homage to Marie Antoinette's powdered tresses), the still popular *"caca d'oie"* ("goose excrement" sounds more elegant in French), and "Isabelle" (an off-white shade recalling la Católica's vow not to change her linen until her consort's return). In the 1940s, the Anglo-American decorator Nancy Lancaster returned to mine this rich vein of inspiration, from which she extracted several nuggets: *"caca du dauphin," "vomitesse de la reine,"* and "elephant's breath."

The repertory of organic substances used in coloration remained relatively stable from the Middle Ages through the late eighteenth century, when the first mineral dyes were discovered, followed some fifty years later by synthetic coal-tar products. It was the individual artisan's skill rather than an abundance of ingredients which determined the bloom of a specific hue. Red seems to have been the color of choice to signal nobility, power, or merely colossal wealth. The bourgeois in Nantes and Rouen were fined for wearing red, limited to members of the aristocracy. One of the earliest tinctures, prized by the ancient peoples of the Mediterranean, was Tyrian purple, the Phoenicians' indelible trademark crimson distilled from the glands of shellfish. Subsequently, it was replaced by cochineal, associated during the Renaissance with the famed "Venetian scarlet," and the versatile madder, which, combined with a mordant, or chemical fixative, generated a spectrum ranging from palest

A fragment of a silk hanging executed for Louis XV's father-in-law, from a design attributed to Philippe de Lasalle, ca. 1760.

salmon to black. (The only natural coloring not dependent on mordants is indigo, which develops a full palette of blues directly—and economically—upon contact with oxygen.)

Yarn is dyed either before spinning or before weaving; coarse textiles may be tinted in the piece. The techniques employed to apply designs to fabrics are far more diverse. The most archaic is probably block printing, based on the same principle as the woodcut. A design is carved into a small panel; the areas in relief are coated with dye; then the block is pressed against the fabric. According to Pliny, the Egyptians had mastered this method by the first century A.D. In 1752, copperplate printing, based on engraving, improved on this process by using etched metal rather than wood as the medium, thus making finer details possible. Flat plates were soon superseded by rollers, which guaranteed the same degree of precision while eliminating awkward intervals between repeats of the motif. The final major innovation in the field was screen printing, introduced just before World War I, in which ink is squeezed *through* a patterned screen, rather than transferred from a block or plate.

Discharge printing is a traditional method of bleaching color out of previously dyed textiles to create designs; the cleared areas may be left gray, or stained another shade. The opposite occurs in resist or reserve dyeing, widespread in Southeast Asia, India, and Africa, where the pattern is defined before color is applied, and in some instances before the yarn is woven. In batik, the motifs are first outlined in wax, then dipped in dye; the wax "resists" the color and is later washed away. Tightly tied sections of

PRECEDING PAGES, LEFT: *Variations on a theme of Chinese Szechuan hand-discharge-dyed fabrics, one of the most famous examples of Chinese traditional blue prints.* PRECEDING PAGES, RIGHT: *Indigo-dyed ikats by Shyam Ahuja, India.*

RIGHT: *Designer Christian Astuguevieille employs the traditional Japanese art of furoshiki to envelop books, boxes, presents, or other fabrics in antique Indonesian batiks.*

fabric or thread resist the dye in the tie-dyeing method. Plangi is tie-dyed cloth; ikat is cloth woven from tie-dyed warp and/or weft. Eighteenth-century French silk manufacturers adapted this process to create the hazy, quasi-impressionistic effect known as *chiné en branche*. In England, the poetically descriptive term for these fabrics was "clouds."

Cloth may also be processed to produce a special texture or finish. Goffering (from the French for "waffle"), compressing the fabric between engraved rollers, creates a sculpted surface. The watered appearance of moiré results from running a folded ribbed fabric through two heated cylinders. The crisp glaze of chintz comes from calendering, in the past with a paper-thin layer of wax, today with resin. The dimpling of seersucker, the blistering of *cloqué*, the see-through effect of *dévoré*, are now all achieved by chemical means. Laboratories have developed invisible protection against wrinkles, stains, and shrinkage, as well as permanent creasing, starching, and waterproofing.

Fashion and Furnishing

The differentiation between fabrics used in furnishing and those for clothing emerged only toward the end of the sixteenth century. Medieval manuscript illuminations, the paintings of the van Eyck brothers and Rogier van der Weyden, the frescoes of Benozzo Gozzoli and Simone Martini, Bronzino's portraits (to cite only the most obvious examples), document the versatility of even highly distinctive fabrics: canopies and corsages were cut from the same stuffs, without any variation in scale, color, or pattern. Garment makers' hunger for innovation

LEFT: *In the Musée Condé in Chantilly, France, the walls, ceilings, and doors of the Grande Singerie are decorated with Chinese and monkey designs dating from the first half of the eighteenth century. The chairs, still covered in their original silk, were part of the furniture of Marie Antoinette's* cabinet de toilette *at Versailles.* RIGHT: *Two brocaded lampas borders, woven for the queen's bedroom at Versailles. Originally woven in 1785, this silk was reproduced by Tassinari, beginning in 1945.*

was the same centuries ago as it is today, with presentations of new textile collections every six months. Through the eighteenth century, however, in the grandest European households, upholstery was still a precious commodity (even Marie Antoinette's trousseau included furnishing fabrics), and was generally replaced no more than twice a generation. Still, the cost of the interiors often rivaled that of the exterior. The memoirist Saint-Simon pitied the henpecked noblemen at the Sun King's court, ruined by their wives' "passion for brocade."

Soft furnishings—clothing for furniture—are still linked to fashion. The Victorians developed this elementary concept ad absurdum, primly concealing with frills and ruffles every potentially indecent, limblike element in the home, from piano legs to balusters. Contemporary preference goes to bare, sleek lines accentuated (rather than dissimulated) by minimal draping and skillful tailoring. Throughout history, fashion has flourished in the face of prohibitive cost or legal restrictions. As soon as the elitist bloom of style becomes generally ac-

cessible, it withers. Nostalgia and novelty are the twin poles between which all modes oscillate. In the domain of the decorative arts, nostalgia generally exerts the stronger pull, if only because a certain timelessness and durability are required wherever expense and wear and tear are high: furniture is meant to last. Charles Percier, the early nineteenth-century French architect, summed up this school of thought when he advocated the "judicious use of those elements hallowed by custom and taste."

Show and Tell

Home is where the heart is, and personal environment is inextricably bound to state of mind in most cultures. Even the least homebound of peoples—nomadic tribes—re-create familiar surroundings in unfamiliar territory by decorating each new site with carefully preserved ancestral textiles. In a well-calculated publicity move (not unlike President Nixon's reference to his wife's good Republican cloth coat), the emperor Augustus made much of using fabrics

ABOVE: *A cotton from a Rouen factory depicting the marriage of Napoleon III to Marie-Eugénie de Montijo.*
RIGHT: *A silk velvet designed for the Holy Year in Rome, 1900.*

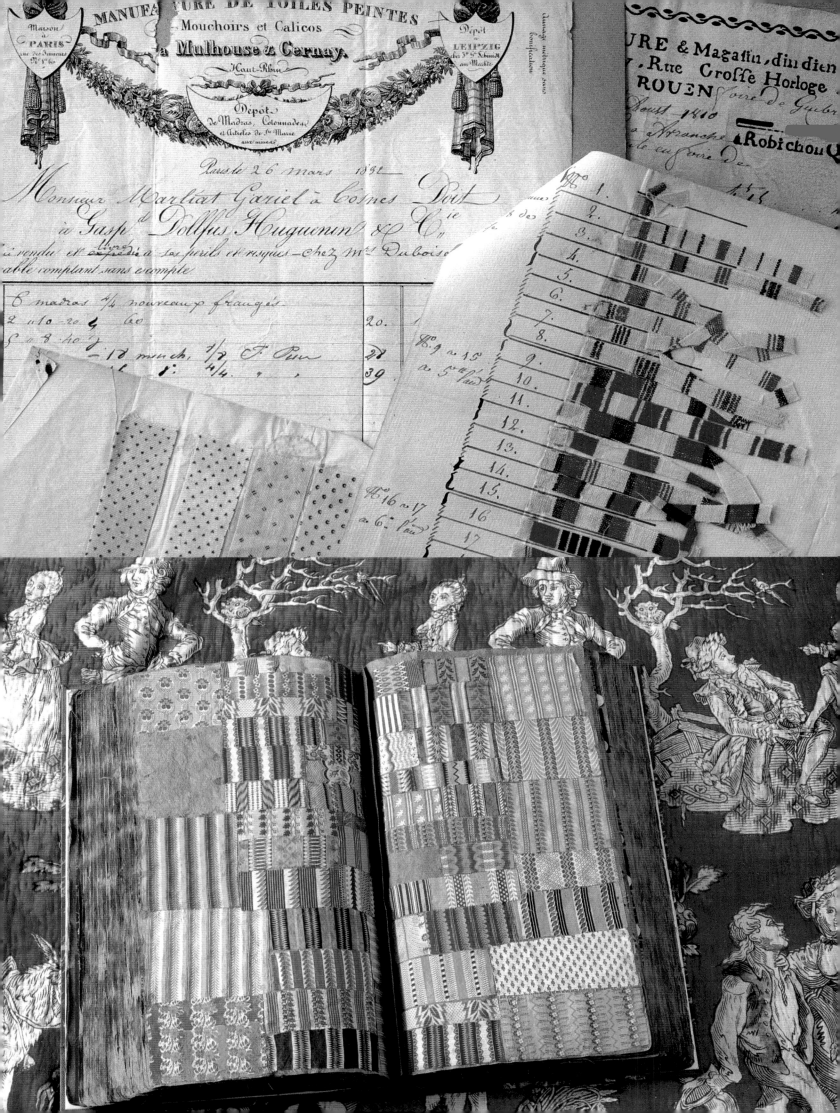

exclusively woven by spouse, sister, and daughter; even today the court weavers of Bhutan distinguish between "heart-woven" textiles and those "woven for sale." Marriageable girls in some remote peasant communities continue to spin and weave the linens for their hope chests, even though equivalent (or superior) ready-made, manufactured items may be had more cheaply in the shops.

Many textiles are to some degree "public" artifacts: often on display, widely disseminated, in the past they were ideal vectors for spreading political, genealogical, or religious information. Yesterday's heraldic and ecclesiastical banners and garments, for example, had the impact of today's advertising logos. In imperial China, the use of specific motifs (the dragon, the sun and moon) and colors (particularly yellow) reflected the subtleties of dynastic hierarchy. A sixteenth-century Persian silk lampas portraying Georgian prisoners of war—men, women, and children—held on leashes by their Safavid captors carried a powerful message. An 1853 toile de Jouy print featuring Napoleon III's marriage to Marie-Eugénie de Montijo exemplifies a milder propaganda, the harbinger of recent tea towels celebrating royal marriages and historic sites.

....

ABOVE LEFT: *Accounts, invoices, and samples from the Musée de l'Impression sur Etoffes'
library collection.* BELOW LEFT: *Fabrics are meticulously grouped together according to color and pattern
in the pages of this sample book, ca. 1820.* ABOVE: *Tiny samples of printed velvet.*

....

FOLLOWING PAGES, LEFT: *The fabulous collection of sample books belonging to the Musée de l'Impression
sur Etoffes in Mulhouse.* FOLLOWING PAGES, RIGHT: *In the Musée Charles Demery in Tarascon,
the attic houses a collection of almost 40,000 printing blocks, miraculously preserved through two centuries—
a priceless design resource inherited by the present Demery generation.*

Négresse battant le Coton
au lieu de le carder.

Conservation

Textile life span depends more on conditions of usage and storage than on actual fiber composition. Airtight Egyptian pyramids have yielded perfectly preserved gauzelike linens; rare sixth-century Byzantine silks, still supple and glowing, encase seldom seen relics in church treasuries from Rome to Sens. Paradoxically, other stuffs have survived as a result of their mutilation: after the collapse of the Ch'ing Dynasty in 1912, for example, callous Occidental hands converted precious hangings sold off by impoverished nobles into seat cushions, piano shawls, and elements of fancy dress. Design books, engraved plates, and rollers—many now conserved in museums—also document the vicissitudes of taste over the last several hundred years. Unfortunately, great swatches of this iconographical reserve were obliterated by the routine wartime practice of confiscating old copper cylinders to manufacture weapons. In France, where the finest printed textiles have been produced since the eighteenth century, historical pattern books and order ledgers, together with original printing blocks, have been preserved in the archives of the Musée Charles Demery in Tarascon, the Musée de la Toile de Jouy, and the Musée de l'Impression sur Etoffes in Mulhouse, as well as in many other collections, both institutional and private.

The Seamy Side

Exploitation and pollution are the two ugly handmaidens of the textile industry. The exploitation of nimble infant fingers in sweatshops from Delhi to Mexico City is nothing new. The Lyons silk business regularly engaged orphan labor; and the Lancashire mills carted young paupers up from London to man the machines. Each new invention devised to increase production—particularly the flying shuttle, spinning jenny, and Jacquard loom—inevitably decreased employment, thus provoking workers' riots and strikes. The interdependence of the American cotton crop and slavery, supported by Western trade with Africa, is of course the most brutish example of human bondage to the bottom line. Inhumanity can also take the indirect route. In the past, the processing of flax devastated pastures and tainted streams throughout northern Europe; now, the environment is threatened by contamination from chemicals used in processing and dyeing, as well as a massive piling up of nonbiodegradable discarded fabrics.

Despite the disfigurements wrought upon her, Nature remains naked, whereas our individual, mostly indoor worlds come fully clothed. Textiles form the backdrop—familiar or changing—of our daily lives. Tickling at least three of our senses, fabrics guarantee basic physical comfort and discomfort, from the convenience of color-coding in public places and the muffled luxury of sound-absorbent wall hangings to the irritating static of synthetic drapes. But the psychological reward can be even greater: the mood-enhancing effects of a mere lampshade, carefully chosen, are known to all. Richard Wagner changed the decor in his study each time he started a major new composition. And when William Cowper penned the elliptical line "I sing the sofa," he struck a cozy chord that has reverberated in sitting rooms down the ages.

CLOCKWISE FROM ABOVE LEFT: *"Paddy and His Companion," an engraving depicting the brutal conditions under which children in the textile industry often were forced to work, London, 1848. "Terrible Accident at a Mill in Lille" in the north of France, 1898. "Cotton Fields in Georgia: the Harvest," an engraving by Riou, 1876. "Negress Beating the Cotton Instead of Carding It," Senegal, a French engraving, from approximately 1810.*

FOLLOWING PAGES: *Elisabeth Garouste and Mattia Bonetti's Topkapi sofa, upholstered in red and gold damask.*

part 1

the *fabrics*

Cotton was occasionally boycotted during the nineteenth century as a product of slavery, but its low cost and convenience rendered it—whether indigenous or imported—essential in most climates. After the turn of the century, Mahatma Gandhi, the founder of modern India, saw cotton as the means of emancipation. He urged his countrymen to free themselves from colonial exploitation by producing their own handspun cotton fabrics. In 1921 the *chakra*—India's traditional spinning wheel—was included in the design of the flag of the National Congress; a stylized version is still incorporated in that of the Indian republic.

The Indus Valley was one of the birthplaces of cotton (the other was Peru). Textile remnants found at the site of Mohenjo-Daro prove that cotton was produced there as early as the second millennium B.C. Local skill in tinting, based on the use of mordants, was renowned: early Latin versions of the Old Testament described wisdom as "more enduring than the dyed colours of India." Some

Cotton

rare Bengal muslins were painted with "invisible" tinctures, programed to appear gradually with the passage of time. *Nebula* and *venti* were delicate Indian weaves especially prized by the ancient Romans, of a texture so diaphanous that they were compared to clouds and wind (they may also have been made of linen). Marco Polo wrote that Coromandel Coast cottons were "the most handsome and the finest in the world." The names of some fabrics still popular today, such as calico and madras, derive from the names of the Indian cities where they were first manufactured.

Cotton slowly but surely circled the world. From India its cultivation spread to the Persian Gulf, then to Egypt and the Mediterranean; Islamic traders introduced it to Africa. The Chinese farmed cotton, followed by the Koreans, whose methods were adopted by the Japanese during the sixteenth century. Although North American Indians began growing cotton sometime between A.D. 700 and 1000, much of the New World's economy rested on the plantation system developed during the colonial period, and ultimately on the slave trade. Vessels loaded with European cloth and trinkets sailed from Liverpool or Bristol for African ports, where they exchanged their merchandise for human cargo, which in turn was trafficked for cotton, tobacco, and sugar in America, to be sold on the Continent.

Throughout history, cotton has successfully been mixed with other fibers. The original Indian gingham was made by combining cotton with silk; later, in the West, cotton woven with linen produced utilitarian crashes, fustians, cretonnes, and dimities. Blends became increasingly popular, of necessity, during the "cotton famine," when the Civil War cut off supplies to the northern United States and Europe. Today, synthetics and polyesters are commonly employed to reinforce cottons used in upholstery. The American designer Jack Lenor

Larsen devised a best-of-both-worlds mix by crossing an Egyptian cotton warp with two wefts, of goat hair and Lurex gimp.

Although cotton is regarded as a handy and serviceable daytime fabric, in Europe brilliantly hued Indian imports were once preferred even to the finest silks: not only were they exotic, and therefore stylish, they were colorfast even when washed. The first *toiles peintes* (which in fact were painted and/or printed) are believed to have been unloaded in France at Marseilles during Henry III's reign. Several decades later the fabled East India Company was granted permission to bring chintzes, painted "callicoes," or pintados into England. European textile merchants quickly realized that greater returns could be obtained if the Indian cottons were designed according to Western taste. Initially, this meant neater compartmentalization, tidier bouquets of blooms familiar to European eyes, and lighter grounds. One English patron complained to a shipper about quilts "with sad red grounds, which are not equally sorted to please all buyers." In both countries, the craze for "Indian goods" was only barely kept in check by protective legislation.

Houses were searched, and offending upholstery was torn off walls and furniture. Calcutta hangings in actor David Garrick's Hampton villa were confiscated by British Customs four years after they had been installed (now they may be admired at London's Victoria and Albert Museum). But no prohibition could entirely eliminate the vogue for patterns we now call paisley, based on the shrimp-shaped boteh blossom, or the flowering tree of life rooted in a rocky mound. In 1708, Daniel Defoe noted with dismay that decorated cottons "had crept into our houses; our closets and bedchambers, curtains, cushions, chairs, and at last beds themselves, were nothing but callicoes and Indian stuffs." England, in thrall to legal restrictions until the last quarter of the century, had

A detail of "Penn's Treaty with the Indian," one of the many printed cottons depicting current and historical events in the collection of the Musée de l'Impression sur Etoffes, Mulhouse.

no heroine like the Marquise de Pompadour, Louis XV's manipulative mistress and unofficial minister of fashion, who is generally credited with the lifting of the French ban in 1759.

Local workshops rapidly entered into competition with the foreign makers. In 1648, enterprising card-printers at Marseilles adapted the techniques of their craft to textile tinting. Wooden blocks, similar to those used to decorate playing cards, were engraved with simple "Indian" motifs, coated in dye, and stamped onto cotton. For some time the intricacies of permanent color eluded these pioneers, but eventually they became skilled enough to combine two and even three tints successfully. An atelier was established in Avignon in 1677; others sprang up throughout Provence. Less than one hundred years later, Marseilles alone boasted twenty-four master *indienneurs*.

The tradition of *indiennage* survives in the deservedly famous Souleiado prints of southern France, which have created what amounts to a new international style in interior decoration. Souleiado, which in Provençal dialect describes a ray of sun breaking through the thunderheads, is produced in Tarascon, a small town on the river Rhône. The factory, which has been operating continuously since the late eighteenth century, possesses an impressive stock of 40,000 printing blocks. Although the cottons are no longer entirely hand-tinted (as they were until 1960), flights of chromatic fancy leaven Souleiado's occasionally pedantic reliance on historic patterns. Their pungent indigos, russets, and golds seem to reflect the colors of the Midi, with its red earth and broom-covered hills caught between sea and sky.

Throughout their stone-built home at Roussillon in the Vaucluse, Dorothée and Jean d'Orgeval—both passionate collectors—display such patinated antique Provençal cottons. Plain white, patterned, and candy-striped fabrics hang on the walls, at windows, across doorways; closets, drawers, and steamer trunks swing open to reveal brightly lined interiors. The overflow is stacked in vast rustic cupboards for easy reference. Exquisitely stitched, reversible *boutis* with arresting combinations of prints and hues serve as coverlets or tablecloths.

Drumcondra, in County Down, was the unlikely setting for one of the great advances in fabric decoration. Like the French *indienneurs* before him, the Irish manufacturer Francis Nixon borrowed a page from the printers' book. In 1752 he hit upon the idea of substituting the small wood blocks employed to stamp motifs on cloth with large copper plates similar to those used for engraved reproductions on paper. The results had, in Nixon's words, "all the advantages of light and shade in the strongest and most lasting colors." Due to the size of the plates (measuring about one meter), the repeats were longer and therefore more smoothly arranged. Thirty years later, Thomas Bell introduced the engraved copper roller: although the repeats were considerably shorter (since the circumference of the cylinders rarely exceeded 50 centimeters), there were now no gaps or overlaps in the patterning.

Copperplate printing achieved its greatest triumphs across the Channel, primarily at the factory that Christophe-Philippe Oberkampf founded in 1760 at Jouy-en-Josas, a village on the outskirts of Paris. The cotton *toiles* produced at Jouy gave their name to a textile genre whose popularity continues unabated to this day. After replacing his original pear and linden wood blocks first by plates and then by roller machines in 1797, Oberkampf was able to turn out 5,000 yards of printed cloth a

RIGHT: *Two contemporary prints in cotton produced by Souleiado.*

FOLLOWING PAGES: *A bedroom in Jean and Dorothée d'Orgeval's house in Roussillon.*
An antique toile de Nantes coverlet graces the bed, while a floral antique boutis *hangs at its head.*
A tiny frill puts the finishing touch to the border flounces of the striped dust covers.

day. Soon his factory was staffed with 1,300 workers, one fourth of whom were qualified draftsmen, engravers, and dyers. Their various activities were delightfully portrayed by one of the stars in the Jouy firmament, Jean-Baptiste Huet. His early design entitled "*Les Travaux de la Manufacture*" depicted not only laborers joyously attending to their tasks in pastoral environs, but the artist himself bent over a drawing board—all under the benevolent supervision of Oberkampf *père* and his infant son.

The "exceedingly pretty" posies and songbirds once favored by Nixon increasingly gave way to more ambitious, didactic subjects. Everything everywhere was grist for the Oberkampf mill, and the quality of Jouy draftsmanship was consistently high: after Huet, Pinelli, Vernet, and Lebas also created patterns agreeable to generation after generation. Toile de Jouy has justly been dubbed "a picture book" documenting the achievements, pleasures, and preoccupations of an era. In addition to the four seasons, elements, and corners of the world, the Holy Sacraments, and famous monuments, the cottons were decorated with fashionable chinoiseries, copies of recently discovered Pompeiian paintings (the "Love Vendor" with her basket of squirming cherubs), subjects from literature (including La Fontaine's *Fables*, Ovid's *Art of Love*, *Paul et Virginie* by Jacques-Henri Bernardin de Saint-Pierre), mythology (particularly the amorous affairs of the gods), and history (Joan of Arc, Henry IV). Current events provided the most edifying examples: "noble savages" abounded, and young America was shown rendering grateful homage to France.

A few decades later, France boasted some

....

LEFT: *A Restoration chair upholstered in a toile de Nantes called "Moses Rescued from the Waters," which represents a meticulous reproduction of two paintings by Nicolas Poussin. Copperplate printed ca. 1825.*
RIGHT: *An example of a printed cotton design from the Zipelius Studio in Alsace, ca. 1827–1840.*

....

FOLLOWING PAGES: *The walls, bed, and chairs of a bedroom at the Château de Bagatelle are upholstered in a cotton printed with a classic pastoral design.*

This sofa in the Musée de Toile de Jouy is covered in a toile de Rouen called "La Côte d'Amour" after a small locality in Normandy. Other cushions are covered in fragments of "Hommage de l'Amérique à la France" and of "Les Quatres Parties du Monde," a design by J. B. Huet, in which the priestess burning incense and surrounded by animals represents Asia.

300 toile manufacturers. The main centers were Rouen, Mulhouse, and Nantes, which by 1785 had nine factories. Of these, the Petitpierre establishment was reputed for its bucolic scenes as well as copies of celebrated artworks. Although his printing technique and design details were less polished than Oberkampf's, Petitpierre could not be matched when it came to quantity: he marketed three times as many patterns as the Jouy-en-Josas firm. A dozen companies were competing in Rouen at the same time, and almost twice as many at Mulhouse. Scenes featuring capably modeled figures and touches of bright color applied by wood block were the trademark of Alsatian fabrics. Sumptuously printed cotton velvets were a specialty during the first half of the nineteenth century: a variety of overlaid tints gave the patterns depth and luster.

By the twentieth century, cotton had become the most democratic of textiles. Although the finest long-staples can still be dearer than some silks, cotton is the natural fabric bringing the broadest range of designs to the greatest number of households at the lowest possible cost. Jouy retains its popularity, and new firms —starting with the revival of block-printed *toiles de Rambouillet* in the 1920s—have resurrected old favorites. Figurative patterns with historical connotations are perennial best-sellers in the conservative world of interior decoration.

The challenge of coloring cotton has always intrigued the textile industry, which has repeatedly attempted to bypass or abbreviate elaborate and costly dyeing processes. In 1915 a Reuters news bulletin declared that the United States would shortly be freed of its dependence on imported German dyestuffs: a Southern planter had succeeded in producing a cotton ranging in color from white to deep olive-green. Furthermore, he was "positive that black cotton, sought for ages by spinners and manufacturers, is about to become a reality." The Australian singer Olivia Newton-John announced in 1991 that her Koala Blue fashion company would soon use "fabrics grown from colored cotton—a natural dye grown in the ground." An American jeans company has already achieved the effect: the first ecologically correct "green" denim is brown.

ABOVE: *Fragment of an antique Persian-style printed cotton.* RIGHT: *"Neptune," one of a series of designs by the painter Raoul Dufy for a collection called "Toiles de Tournon," done for the celebrated firm Bianchini Férier for which Dufy worked between 1912 and 1928.*

LEFT: *A sample book of linen damask weaves and skeins of different qualities of linen thread produced in Flanders at the beginning of the century.* ABOVE: *In Christian Astuguevieille's Paris apartment, a heady pile of classic linen tea towels tops one of his corded urns.*

Linen and cotton are both "intimate" fabrics—popularly recommended for use not only against the skin but also in the private parts of the home: bedroom, boudoir, kitchen, bath. Made from cellulose fibers, both are absorbent, pliable, lightweight—that is, ideal for practical service or informal settings. Of the two, linen is almost certainly the more ancient: scraps of twined flax have been excavated in Neolithic settlements.

Cleanliness is next to godliness, and linen has traditionally been associated with both concepts. From antiquity through the Enlightenment, wearing (and changing) linen garments was advocated not merely as a measure of hygiene but as protection against illness. The department store category "lingerie" derives from the Latin name for the flax plant, *linum*. Today, the generic term "linens" still conjures up an array of pristine household accessories.

In various early Mediterranean cultures, linen carried religious connotations. Herodotus and Pliny described its manufacture in

Linen

Egypt, known as the land of flax, where priests' raiment was made exclusively of linen (wool was disregarded as "lifeless debris from an unclean animal"). According to mythology, the goddess Isis, patroness of the Afterworld, invented linen in order to fashion graveclothes for her brother and spouse, Osiris. The workshops of the Nile Delta became famous for a particularly iridescent quality of linen cloth, whose colors changed with the time of day. The Hebrews too prized flax for its purity: the Bible says that the Tabernacle was hung with "ten curtains of fine twined linen, and blue, and purple, and scarlet."

Arachne's mythical superiority to Athena in weaving has sometimes been attributed to the fact that the Lydian woman may have used fine linen thread instead of coarse yarn. The Greeks and Romans both produced linen in limited quantities, but it never formed a significant staple of their textile industries, which were wool-based. Linen's applications were primarily utilitarian, due to its properties of resilience and absorbency. Sails, circus awnings, rope, even scrolls, were made of linen.

Although the Romans are known to have encouraged the cultivation of flax in their transalpine provinces, Phoenician traders were also responsible for promoting the manufacture of linen in northern Europe during the first millennium B.C. By 200 B.C. all Gaul was, in the words of Plautus, "covered with flax." After the fall of the empire, the barbarian hordes thundering across Europe dealt destruction to the textile industry. Under Charlemagne, however, each family unit was required to produce its own linen; Charles the Fat went one step farther, ordering ninth-century princesses of

....

LEFT: *In La Chambre de Retrait at Leeds Castle in Kent, England, a simple wooden cooper's tub is surrounded with a fine white linen curtain suspended from a sparver canopy. The linen towels that line the tub protected the royal bather from the rough wood. A linen-draped stool was placed inside the bath for the queen to sit on and another beside it to assist her in stepping in and out.*
RIGHT: *In Paris, Agnes Comar uses white embroidery and crystal palm drops on natural linen bed hangings.*

from Cambrai. Before the technical advances of this century, the processing of linen could take almost a year, from sowing the seed to finishing the cloth—a veritable gestation. Despite picturesque tales of wee folk and hobgoblins who spun and wove in the twinkling of an eye, linen making was not only arduous but potentially harmful to both workers as well as the environment. The bleaches used to cleanse the fibers polluted the fields and poured into the rivers; weavers were prone to their own occupational ailment, asthma.

Like silk, linen was almost literally worth its weight in gold. In 1394 a prisoner held by the Turks was ransomed with bolts of linen. Emperor Charles V had "no fears for Flanders as long as its fields will bear flax." According to a French seventeenth-century document, "Linen cloths are the true gold and silver mines of this kingdom, because they are developed only to be transported to countries where gold and silver are obtained."

The use of linen in upholstery is hardly a novelty: in the fourteenth century Pope John XXII's chambers in the palace at Avignon were hung with fabric imported from Florence. Today the textile industry is promoting linen as a wall covering: it remains stable even when exposed to extreme temperature changes, and its acoustic insulation has been estimated as high as 80 percent. Linen velvets, shantungs, and printed and self-patterned weaves are available in several widths. In the home, however, linen is still used mainly for bedclothes and summer slipcovers; glass curtains are cut from the lightest quality, batiste. For many decades "no-iron" has been the proud watchword on most household fabric tags; it is hard for our eye to reaccustom itself to the nonchalant charm of deeply wrinkled cases, which suggest to us the loss of constant domestic vigilance.

the blood to learn to spin and weave. Less than two centuries later, William the Conqueror's wife Matilda embroidered a linen canvas—incorrectly referred to as the Bayeux tapestry—with her husband's exploits.

Although flax was grown from Ireland to the Russian shores of the Baltic, Flanders, with its humid climate, rich alluvial soil, and long summer days, soon became what it still is: a major linen center. (Belgium is said to take its name from the ancient Celtic word for flax, *belc'h.*) Each important Flemish town supported a citywide manufactory, often producing a distinctive fabric known by its appellation of origin: "diaper," for tablecloths and napkins, came from Ypres, and superfine "cambric"

ABOVE: *The fourposter in Agnes Comar's Paris bedroom is hung with generous pleats of natural linen, spattered with a white embroidered motif and trimmed with crystal palm drops.* RIGHT: *The baroness Guy de Rothschild's bedroom in her New York apartment, ca. 1984. The walls and curtains are of floral linen, which decorator Geoffrey Bennison copied from a nineteenth-century fragment discovered in a noble nursery.*

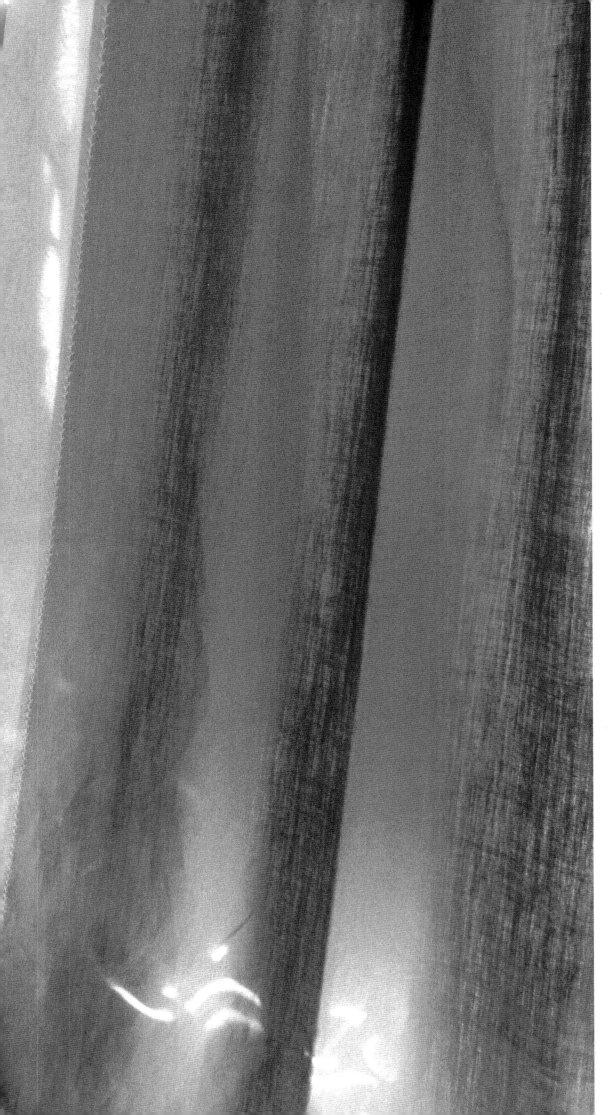

LEFT: *Designer Agnes Comar uses natural linen trimmed with white organza for the curtains of a tent, which enclose a chair covered with embroidered linen. The cushions, in natural and white linen, are fastened by simple raffia laces.*

FOLLOWING PAGES: *The chamber of the mistress of the household in Gripsholm Castle, Mariefred, Sweden. The room was refurbished in the 1890s with simple linen bed hangings, pillows, and chair seats, and is said to have been a source of inspiration to the wife of painter Carl Larsson for the interior of their family home.*

"The shadow of the mulberry is the shadow of gold," according to a secular Italian adage which summarizes the silk industry from botany to benefits. Silk originated in a specific geographical area, the Chinese province of Shantung, where it was manufactured in limited quantities and marketed to the world only through designated channels. An internationally prized commodity, it could be used to pay taxes in the Celestial Empire or to ransom Rome from the Goths. Until the modern era, a country's wealth could almost be measured in rolls of silk, whether produced or purchased.

To maintain product exclusivity and protect their assets, the Chinese successfully limited access to all phases of sericulture to the imperial entourage for almost three millennia. Westerners long believed that the Chinese harvested silk fibers from the bast of rare, indigenous trees. The earliest documented traces of silk are remote: at a site in southern Shansi, archeologists excavated a cocoon that had been cut open in Neolithic times. Legend tells of Hsi-Ling-Shi, the wife of Emperor Huang-Ti, who unintentionally discovered the silkworm's secret when she accidentally dropped a cocoon into her steaming tea bowl and fished out a long and supple filament. Until abolished by Sun Yat-sen in 1911, Hsi-Ling-Shi's

Silk and Velvet

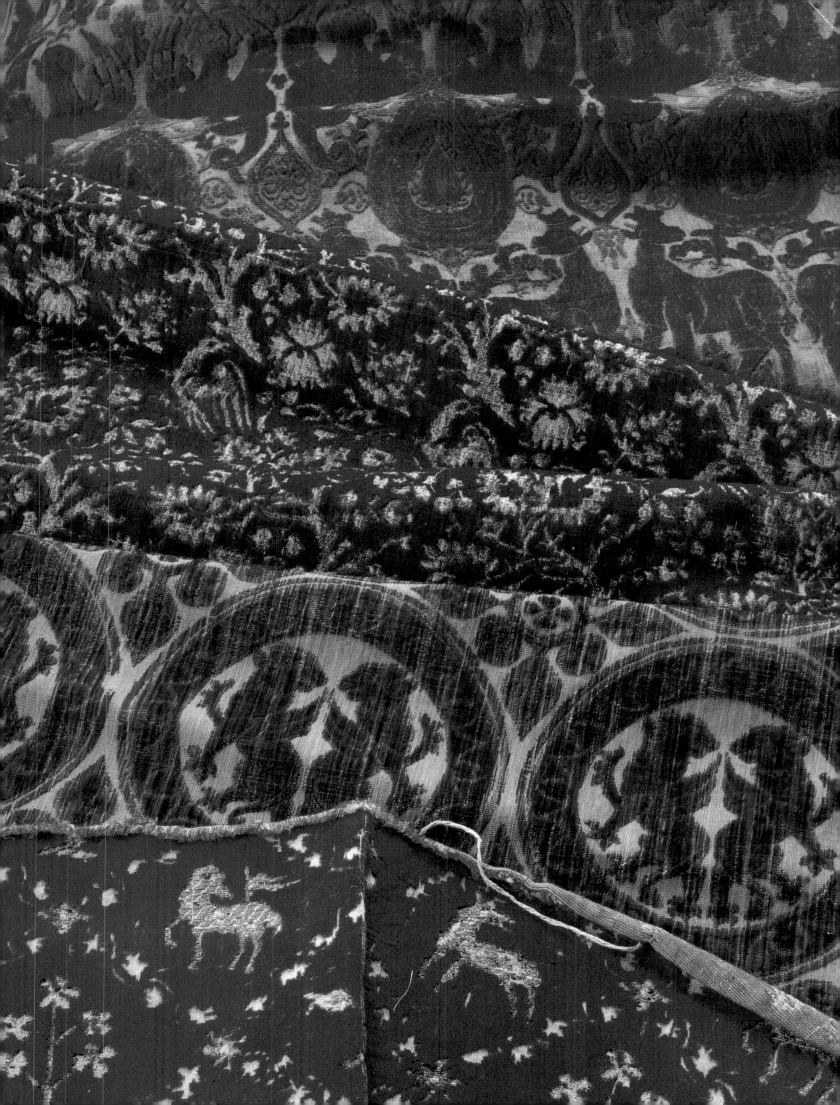

feast day was celebrated each spring with offerings of the silkworm's favored mulberry leaves.

By the Han era (206 B.C.–A.D. 221), the silk trade had become so important that the combination of overland and maritime routes connecting China to commercial centers on the Mediterranean, Red Sea, and Indian Ocean had become known as the Great Silk Road. Even in antiquity, China was not the only source of silk, but Chinese silk was the finest in both texture and color. According to Aristotle and Pliny, silk—probably wild—was worked on the Greek island of Cos, associated with cults of the goddesses Athena and Demeter. India was also famous for its yellow-tinged silk; it was woven from short fibers because the trick of boiling, then unwinding the cocoons to obtain a single continuous filament was unknown there. A more flattering explanation has it that the Indians chose not to destroy the butterfly out of respect for life: they preferred to allow it to emerge alive from the cocoon, thus tearing the long strands.

The mystery of silk manufacture was eventually unraveled. Mythology, as ever, held women responsible. There was the princess betrothed to the ruler of Khotan who, before her departure to the Mongol kingdom, concealed silkworm eggs in her elaborate headdress. There was the "golden-haired maiden" who fled the persecution of her mother-in-law to Japan, where she providentially turned into a cocoon. There were the concubines taken hostage and successfully interrogated by Koreans on behalf of the Japanese.

In reality, industrial espionage began in A.D. 552 with Emperor Justinian, who sent a pair of Nestorian monks on a mission to the Orient. They returned to Constantinople with their hollow bamboo canes filled with *Bombyx mori*

eggs and mulberry seeds. The Nestorians became imperial cloth manufacturers, producing resplendent silks in imperial ateliers exclusively for courtiers and foreign potentates—the only customers who could afford such luxury. Today, the $200 price tag on a Hermès silk square might seem outrageous, but it has been calculated that a 9-ounce length of purple silk cost up to the equivalent of $23,000 in Constantinople.

As the Arab campaign unfurled around the Mediterranean, state-controlled *tiraz* (palace factories) were staffed with local weavers: Byzantine, Coptic, Syrian, and Sassanian. Many modern textile terms may be traced to this period of Muslim domination, including muslin (referring to the city of Mosul), damask (Damascus), ormesine (Hormuz), and taffeta (from *tafta,* meaning woven). Royal factories were also founded farther afield, in Spain and most notably in Sicily. The Norman conquest of the island fostered the development of a textile tradition distinguished by fantastical heraldic motifs. In 1147, King Roger II imported to Palermo Greek artisans who grafted Byzantine elements onto the established Saracen manner. All European silk weaving evolved out of the hybrid Sicilian school.

After the Angevin invaders lost Sicily to the Aragonese in the thirteenth century, Palermitan weavers scattered to the Italian peninsula, where many settled in Lucca. This Tuscan town soon became renowned for its silk *diasprum,* or diasper, a richly patterned lampas so called because of its brilliant jaspery sheen. Magnificent designs of Sicilian derivation, featuring paired birds and quadrupeds, blossoms and starbursts, were sought after by both aristocratic and ecclesiastical patrons.

In Renaissance Florence, the silk industry

was powered by 7,000 looms and over 15,000 workers. Stylized pomegranate, thistle, pinecone, and artichoke motifs are characteristic of the brocades and damasks of this period. By the mid-seventeenth century, Florentine silks had become too rare and costly to compete with French stuffs. The craft was kept alive by special commissions from the Imperial and Royal Court of Tuscany, for precious satin wall hangings described in the makers' inventories as "*ricchissimi e gravissimi*" (most rich and heavy). Many of these draperies still adorn the apartments for which they were originally devised at the Pitti Palace.

The northern ports of Genoa and Venice were equally famed for their silks. In Venice, it was said that to reach perfection silk must pass through sixteen hands, from those of the reeler to those of the merchant. The manufacture of silk, sparked by Marco Polo's travels in Cathay, remained chronically dependent on foreign commerce. In order to keep their looms active year-round, Venetian weavers imported cocoons from the Orient, Sicily, and Spain, as well as raw silk from Persia and Turkey. Foreign textiles enriched the Venetian "image bank" with exotic iconography: trees of life, peonies, and lotus flowers, hippocampi, eagles, leopards, and dragons. Genoa rivaled La Serenissima in the production of elaborately worked velvets: polychrome, figured, voided, goffered, with cut and/or uncut pile. The sumptuous floral *giardiniera* style and *inferriata* patterns, inspired by wrought-iron volutes, were Genoese specialties—as was a plain black velvet of exceptionally even and lustrous finish.

For centuries a Draconian system of incentives and deterrents governed every aspect of Italian sericulture, ensuring output and quality. Textile workers were even forbidden to emigrate: those who disobeyed "could be killed anywhere in the world." Designers were required by contract to refresh "their ideas of good taste in fashion" by regular trips to Paris or Vienna. Professional poaching was widespread. The Venetian ambassador in Spain commented on his own attempt to hire a French weaver away from a Toledo workshop: "The comfort of better premises, of conduct more genteel, and of some greater profit should be strong enough to persuade him to change skies."

The Spanish painter Mariano Fortuny y Madrazo, who came to Venice at the end of the nineteenth century, jolted local velvet manufacturers out of their secular reliance on tradition. Famed as the creator of the delicately pleated columnar Delphos robe, Fortuny also designed furnishing fabrics with an antiquarian flavor. Kaleidoscopic hues, enhanced by an iridescent patina, were the Spaniard's distinctive trademark. Fortuny's heritage is apparent in the contemporary geometric velvets of Norelene, freely inspired by Venetian mosaic and marble inlay decoration.

Redolent of times past, the boldly figured silks of Italy remain the upholstery of choice for formal interiors—or merely to suggest a stately-home ambience.

France became "satin country" by dint of decrees and edicts. Since the Middle Ages, when Parisian ateliers could barely produce sufficient or satisfactory dress trim for the court, foreign silk imports were a drain on the exchequer. Under Louis XI, about half a million ecus were spent annually on Italian fabrics; by the end of the sixteenth century, the amount spent had risen over 7 million. Henry IV, the pragmatic French monarch who opined that Paris was well worth a Mass when he converted to take the throne, attempted to reorganize the industry from the ground up. He ordered approximately

RIGHT, CLOCKWISE FROM TOP RIGHT: *Silk velvet with motifs inspired by the floor mosaics of the Aquileia Basilica, woven on a traditional loom in Venice by Luigi Bevilacqua. Cut velvets are still woven on hand-operated looms in Venice, according to traditional patterns by Rubelli. A reproduction of a Venetian document from the end of the seventeenth century, woven by Rubelli. Two cushions of silk and cotton in the characteristic subtle shades and rich ornamentation of Mariano Fortuny.*

RIGHT: *Mariano Fortuny's studio in Venice forms a perfect backdrop for two of his fabric designs.*
FAR RIGHT: *Detail of the silk taffeta curtains in the former bedroom of the Duchesse de Mouchy in Jacques Garcia's house in Paris. The gilt polonaise bed, reflected in the mirror, is signed* Jacob *and is also dressed in silk taffeta.*

ABOVE LEFT: *"Crimean Campaign."* This hanging satin brocade was executed for Catherine the Great of Russia to celebrate the conquest of the Crimea by Potemkin in 1783. The design is attributed to Philippe de Lasalle, the designer-manufacturer considered to be the greatest textile artist of the eighteenth century. ABOVE RIGHT: *"Gros de Tour broché."* This silk masterpiece was originally executed for the summer furnishings of Marie Antoinette's apartment at Versailles by Desfarges in 1786–87. (A detail of the coordinated border appears on page 25.)

10 million mulberries planted in Provence, and in 1602 he even uprooted the venerable royal domains of the Tuileries and Fontainebleau to accommodate more bushes.

In 1665, Louis XIV gave Colbert, who had advised him that "the means of keeping gold and silver in your kingdom is to make here that which they make there," carte blanche to reform the French textile industry. A draper's son, Colbert standardized every minute detail of the weaver's craft—from the terms of apprenticeship to the policing of the profession, from the number and tension of warp threads to the acceptable maximum quantity of errors. Although silk factories were inaugurated in other provincial centers, Lyons became known as "La Grande Fabrique," with whole quarters occupied by domestic workshops staffed by families of *canuts*. The provost assured Colbert that local silks equaled Italian materials—with the one exception, he admitted, of Genoese black velvet.

Many technical improvements emerged in this citywide textile laboratory. It is said that Octavio Mey accidentally discovered the process of lustering by drawing a silk thread through his teeth. Patterns—as well as work patterns—were significantly affected by Claude Dangon's 1605 drawloom for figured fabrics, which required the assistance of a drawboy. Two hundred years later, the perfected Jacquard loom, which produced finely contoured designs, retired that same drawboy.

Design was the very soul of the Fabrique, according to one observer; another wrote: "Never forget, O Lyons, that it is your designers who are responsible for the prosperity of your manufactories." The artists who provided

ABOVE LEFT AND ABOVE RIGHT: *Two details of a famous white satin, brocaded in chenille and silk, which was executed by Gilles Gaudin of Lyons in 1788, most probably for the bedroom of a royal household. The magnificent pastoral design of the fabric, incorporating embroidered flowers, musical instruments, birds and bird cages, fruit, and garlands, is frequently attributed to textile artist Philippe de Lasalle. In 1805, the satin was installed in Empress Josephine's bedroom at Fontainebleau.*

patterns to the ateliers were often trained in Paris and encouraged to refresh their repertory through "continuing education." Models for furnishing fabrics were protected for twenty-five years, and copying was at least in theory prohibited. The law severely penalized those breaches of contract referred to as "the infidelity of designers."

Tentatively attributed museum scraps alone testify to the achievements of the first generation of draftsmen: the architectural fantasies and grotesques of Jean Bérain, the classical foliage of Daniel Marot, and the carefully composed bouquets of Androuet du Cerceau.

Two stylistic trends evolved in the early eighteenth century: lace-patterned silks and bizar silks. The former adapted motifs from trim used in upholstery and dressmaking; the latter—as the name implies—displayed strangely elongated, asymmetrical combinations of exotic and familiar motifs.

The challenge of indicating depth in a two-dimensional medium was resolved at Lyons, where, according to reports, Courtois (d. 1750) first "developed the understanding of chiaroscuro to an astonishing degree." His successor, the "Raphael of designers," Jean Revel (1684–1715), invented the *point rentré* by which areas of sharply contrasting color were meshed thread by thread to create the impression of relief. As a result, bloated triumphs of fruit and flowers—with roses like cabbages and olives like pumpkins, in the words of a contemporary wit—gave way to delicately drawn chinoiseries, ribbons and baskets, and garlands of miniature blossoms.

Yet another later "Raphael" was Philippe de La Salle (1723–1805): his Rococo meanders, inhabited by peacocks, doves, and pheasants, were executed for Marie Antoinette at Versailles and for Catherine the Great at Tsarskoye Selo and Petrodvorets. The elegant linear interpretations of the "Etruscan" mode by Jean-Démosthène Dugourc (1749–1825) may still be seen on the walls of the Escorial and Aranjuez palaces in Spain.

The world became acquainted with Lyons, as bolts of silk were sent as prestigious diplomatic gifts to the electress of Brandenburg, the dey of Algiers, the king of Guinea, the ruler of Siam, and the king of Denmark. Casanova and Mozart were customers. Although the Terror momentarily halted manufacturing in Lyons and reduced the market for luxury goods, Napoleon quickly perceived that "treasures and riches could return the State to splendor." His imperial residences, as well as dozens of confiscated properties throughout conquered Europe, were soon refurbished in accordance with the Emperor's terse but demonstrably effective instruction "to do better than in the past."

Prerevolutionary portraits of the great and the good were the first specimens of *tableaux tissés,* or woven pictures, featuring wreathed medallions "of the most exact resemblance." The vogue continued unabated through the nineteenth century with effigies of public personages such as Queen Victoria, Lord Robert Baden-Powell, or Félix Faure. The concept of fabric as a unique, autonomous work of art was reinforced by such ambitious designers as Gaspard Grégoire (1751–1846), whose vast—up to 6 square meters—and exquisitely tinted velvet compositions still force admiration.

The continuity of the Lyons silk tradition is unrivaled. When Prelle bought out Lamy & Giraud, it acquired documents and designs dating back to 1752; Tassinari & Chatel, as the

BELOW LEFT: *Two examples of silk lampas with "grotesque" motifs. Originally inspired by the discovery of the strange and intricate decors of the Emperor Nero's house in Rome, around 1480, these designs remained popular until the end of the nineteenth century.* BELOW RIGHT: *A Greek motif brocade on a satin base, woven for the bedroom of Napoleon's son, the King of Rome.*

successor of the distinguished Pernon and Grand firms, has accumulated three centuries of experience. Heirs to the most complete archives of yesteryear, these manufacturers tap the rich and profitable vein of historical reproductions. Newcomers such as Bianchini-Férier, established in Paris in 1888 before coming to Lyons, instead built their reputation on contemporary design. In a bid to link mass-produced textiles to developments in the visual arts, they signed on prestigious *créateurs*, ranging from Paul Iribe and Raoul Dufy to Henri Soulages and Hans Hartung—as well as the pioneer photographer, Jacques-Henri Lartigue.

The only real threat to the supremacy of Lyons were the Spitalfields workshops. Although London weavers were far from self-sufficient, threading their looms with imported silk from Italy, China, and Persia, they were rich in savoir faire. After the 1685 Act of Revocation outlawing Protestantism in France, almost 100,000 Huguenot textile workers sought asylum across the Channel, bringing with them welcome expertise. Although much of the silk produced in Britain was intended to be worn rather than hung, the great houses of Britain—from Ham to Highclere—are indebted to these "strangers," as they were identified by the natives, for some of their finest and most durable decors. From the eighteenth century, English silks were distinguished by pleasant floral patterns on light grounds. Occasional flights of fancy are documented, such as a bizar silk portraying sprats on a gridiron.

English designers, such as James Leman (1688–1745) and Anna Maria Garthwaite (1689/90–1765), were recognized as imaginative and highly competent, but technical limi-

---

BELOW LEFT: *A polychrome brocatelle in the Gothic style, dated 1853.* BELOW RIGHT: *A silk toile designed by André Groult, a well-known French designer of the Art Deco period.*

FOLLOWING PAGES, LEFT: *A silk taffeta embroidered in chain and Beauvais stitch, late eighteenth century.*
FOLLOWING PAGES, RIGHT: *A polonaise bed dressed in printed silk in Karl Lagerfeld's Paris apartment.*

RIGHT: *A silver brocade border from Napoleon's bedroom in the Grand Trianon, atop the emperor's portrait.* BELOW: *A contemporary silk damask with the traditional Empire bee design, woven by Tassinari & Chatel. Fabrics, furnishings, and ornaments of the Empire often featured the Napoleonic motif—enormous N's encircled by laurel wreaths, eagles, and swans, in addition to bees.* FAR RIGHT: *In the chapel adjoining Spanish decorator Duarte Pinto-Cuelho's palace, rows of red velvet and damask cushions adorn the pews.* BELOW RIGHT: *An intricate silk rep, woven by Bianchini Férier.*

tations within the industry were apparent: in 1760, Horace Walpole noted tartly that "of two colours they make them very well, but they cannot arrive at three." Deficiencies were corrected by pirating information about machinery (the Jacquard loom, watering calenders), as well as designs which the informer was explicitly ordered "to copy as near as you can."

By the mid-nineteenth century, British weavers were reissuing French patterns that had been popular one generation earlier. And in 1900, a reviewer surveying an exhibit of textiles by Warner, Britain's premier silk manufacturer, wrote that "the best of them, it has to be owned, are copies of old works." Today, historical reproductions for exacting clients such as the royal household and the National Trust have in fact become Britain's principal stock in trade.

Although by the early twentieth century the United States produced almost as much silk as France, its quality and design were markedly inferior. The history of sericulture in the New World was fraught with disaster, since Hernán Cortés's ill-fated attempt to breed the silkworm in Mexico in the sixteenth century. During the colonial era, the British briefly established mulberry plantations in Virginia, Georgia, and South Carolina, which they were forced to abandon. Later, promoters of get-rich-quick schemes tried in vain to lay the foundation for a nationwide cottage industry. Religion proved effective when all else failed: the Shaker communities wove handsome, simple-patterned textiles, as did the Mormons in Utah, who in 1855 imported a supply of mulberry seed and *Bombyx mori* eggs directly from France. Although their fertile soil and temperate climate made the Southern states an ideal environment for sericulture, American workers apparently failed to provide the tender loving care required by the silkworm. In Chinese silk farms, loud voices and talk of death were prohibited in the presence of the cocoons.

Fine reproductions have the great virtue of preserving not only historical designs but techniques that have been cast into disuse by totally mechanized thousand-loom factories on a round-the-clock schedule. If it were not for wealthy private or institutional patrons, the old hand-operated *méquiers à bras* would long ago have crumbled into dust. The combination of specialized weavers manipulating 36,000 threads strung on five-hundred-year-old machinery to produce less than an inch of silk fabric a day is simply not cost-effective—although the landmark Setificio San Leucio at Caserta, founded by the Bourbon kings of Naples, is still going strong. Now that the Vatican has curtailed expenditures for ceremonial draperies and liveries, northern European dynasties and museum restoration projects keep Italian and French factories humming. Luigi Bevilacqua of Venice supplied the royal palace in Stockholm, as well as the theater at Drottningholm, with specially woven silk hangings. Another Venetian firm, Rubelli, celebrated for its sumptuous patterned velvets, produces upholstery for La Scala in Milan and the Uffizi and Pitti museums in Florence, as well as the private quarters of Buckingham Palace. The White House commissioned yellow-cut velvet with a staggering 5.85 meter repeat from Tassinari and Chatel. The same firm has just completed a thirty-year order for the upholstery of the Queen's Bedchamber at Versailles.

It has been calculated that during the eighteenth century, at least two hundred kinds of fabrics were made in France. Today, even with the development of a range of synthetic fibers and the extraordinary versatility of industrial methods, the textile business seems bent on verifying that old saw, "Things were better when times were worse."

An antique Portuguese cloth, heavily embroidered with silk motifs, covers a table in Spanish decorator Duarte Pinto-Cuelho's palace drawing room.

LEFT: *A sheep-shearing illustration from a nineteenth-century children's book.* ABOVE: *A fragment of an Egyptian woolen hanging of the sixth century, conserved by the Victoria and Albert Museum in London.*

The Golden Fleece that Jason and his Argonauts bartered for the throne of Iolcus, is a mythological symbol not only of bravery and wealth, but also of power. The Order of the Golden Fleece, instituted by Philip the Good, Duke of Burgundy, in 1429, is still awarded by the Bourbon monarchy of Spain. The woolsack, a squarish bag of wool traditionally placed under the seat of the lord chancellor at the opening of the British House of Lords, is synonymous with the high office itself. For centuries wool was a public emblem of prestige; today it is an extraordinarily serviceable fiber—warm, sturdy, and fire retardant.

Although sheep's wool is the most common, other varieties are made from the pelts of rabbits, bison, llamas, vicuñas, alpacas, guanacos, yaks, and even dogs. Horsehair, in particular, can be woven to make a handsome and durable fabric often used to cover seats. It has become costly since the introduction of the horseless carriage caused the once-plentiful supply to plummet. Horsehair is always reinforced and embellished with colored strands of cotton, linen, silk, or wool: the upholstery of George Washington's

Wool

side chairs in his home at Mount Vernon has a white horsehair weft combined with blue and gold silk warps.

Felt is probably the earliest woolen fabric devised by mankind. Hairs—matted rather than woven—are fulled (by moistening, heating, and then pressing) to form a compact cloth that insulates from heat, cold, and dampness. Felt is still widely employed today: Mongolian nomads use it to make tents, Borsalino hatters shape it into fedoras, and gamblers toss onto it their "rattling dice."

The spinning and weaving of wool developed after that of plant fibers, around five thousand years ago. The two main cloth categories are woolens (with a high nap, made from tough, short-staple fleece) and worsteds (with no nap, made from supple, long-staple fleece). Archeological artifacts prove that ancient wool industries flourished in areas as far removed as the Andean highlands, Egypt, northern Europe, and Asia Minor. Babylon was called the "land of wool." The Hebrews, who were renowned for their woolen fabrics, protected their prize sheep with overcoats; Australian breeders still observe this precaution today.

"She lived chastely, spun wool, and stayed at home" was the Roman definition of a good woman. In addition to encouraging homespun, which represented all the domestic virtues, Rome imported raw wool and cloth from Spain, Gaul, and Africa to be processed in imperial factories throughout the peninsula. Craftsmen's activities are illustrated in the frescoes decorating Pompeiian workshops. The highly efficient system crumbled after the fall of the empire, when textiles became a cottage industry.

Muslim Spain was a great center of sheep raising as well as of wool weaving. The evolution of the merino sheep during the fourteenth century was the outstanding Hispanic contribution to the international wool industry. Louis XVI introduced the fine-fleeced breed to France, as did George III to England; it is believed to have reached the New World shortly after 1800. The pliancy and gossamer texture of merino yarn—almost rivaling that of silk—makes it ideal for the sumptuous yet hard-wearing damask weaves used in upholstery. The rarest category—superfine—with staples so fine that they are almost indistinguishable to the naked eye, can command over $30,000 at auction per 100-kilo bale.

In the British Isles, economic strength was directly related to wool production. First the Roman, then the Norman invaders encouraged farmers to produce their own wool. Guilds were established in the eleventh century, and soon 7 million pounds of wool were being shipped each year to the Continent. "I thank God and ever shall/It is the sheep hath payed for all" was inscribed on the home of a medieval English merchant. Although British artisans were initially less skilled in weaving than the Flemish, and in dyeing than the Italians, they developed goods of such substantial quality that even Erasmus of Rotterdam endorsed them as "the best" to be had in Europe. Britain encouraged sheep farming in its colonies; Australia still

PRECEDING PAGES, LEFT: *Horsehair in its raw state. Long white hair is the most prized and is imported mainly from China and Argentina.* PRECEDING PAGES, RIGHT: *Samples of horsehair cloth woven by the French manufacturer Le Crin, which has been weaving on the same jacquard looms since 1815.*

ABOVE: *An engraving from the* Encyclopédie Diderot et D'Alembert *showing a craftsman sorting the different qualities of wool.* RIGHT: *A wool and silk weave, ca. 1870.*

provides an abundant source of raw material to be transformed into twin sets and tweeds.

Wool and silk were said to be the "two beautiful eyes" of Florence, the textile center of Renaissance Italy. The most powerful Italian confraternity was the Arte della Lana, which in that city alone numbered some 30,000 wool workers producing 80,000 bolts of cloth annually. Another corporation, the Calimala, was famous for finishing—improving—textiles made elsewhere. Tens of thousands of unbleached, roughly woven *panni,* generally imported from Flanders or Britain, were fulled, trimmed, then dyed, before being put back into circulation onto markets in Europe, Asia, or Africa. Since the Calimala was dependent on foreign trade, the guild maintained a network of inns and a postal service for its representatives abroad. At home, carrot-and-stick tactics governed the hierarchy: members could expect to reap a 12 percent profit per annum—but craftsmen could expect to lose their right hands for taking shortcuts.

Charlemagne revived the Roman *gynaeceum,* the workshop staffed by women, and imposed protectionary measures to strengthen the textile industry. By the Middle Ages, France had become the hub of the European wool trade: the fairs in Champagne attracted buyers and vendors from regions both north and south. French fabric production was severely crippled by the effects of the Hundred Years War, compounded by a lack of consistent government support. After the mid-seventeenth century, Louis XIV's comptroller Jean-Baptiste Colbert tackled the wool industry with the same expediency he applied to promoting sericulture. He enticed the talented Flemish weaver Josse van Robais from Holland to Picardy in 1655. The royal atelier he founded in Abbeville was soon

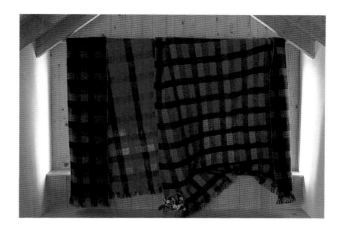

famous not only for its weaves, which were created through an intricate thirty-two–step process, but also for the unprecedented subtlety of its dyes.

The French demand grew for "Holland-style" stuffs, with their ingenious weaves and finishes. Goffered Utrecht velvet, made of worsted or mohair mixed with cotton, was a durable choice for upholstery. The "new draperies" were another Dutch invention which spread rapidly to Britain as well: their pliable textures were the result of combining a woolen weft and a worsted warp (occasionally substituted with linen). One of these fabrics with a upright pile, *mockadoe,* lives on today in the form of moquette. The fashion of employing it not only as carpeting but also for wall hangings dates to the eighteenth century, when Madame de Rohan used it to cover the walls of her Parisian salon in the Hôtel de Soubise.

The fantastic variety of woolen and worsted stuffs available from the 1600s through the turn of the century has today been lost. Though their names have been handed down in wills, manufacturers' ledgers, and dowry and laundry lists, many of the genuine articles did not survive the wear and tear of everyday use. In the colonial United States, families habitually produced their own rugged flannels, shags, and

LEFT: *In writer Paul Duncan's former house in Spitalfields, London, tartan curtains and antique fabrics make an appropriate setting for his Scottish noble origins.* ABOVE: *Traditional woolen plaids from the Orkney islands in northern Scotland.*

FOLLOWING PAGES: *Agnes Comar designed two coverlets and cushions and had them appliquéd in felt for her Paris apartment.*

broadcloths. Other popular weaves, inherited from the Old Country, included serge (the predecessor of denim) and everlasting, related to the English perpetuana. Camlets, such as camleteens, moreens, and cheneys, could be stamped with damask patterns as a substitute for silk. Stout calamanco, often striped, was used for bed hangings. Challis and camel's hair were introduced during the 1900s, along with the evocatively titled albatross, doeskin, brilliantine, and Sicilian.

The cashmere route supplanted the Great Silk Road, when the Kashmir craze blossomed in the West two centuries ago. Ladies of fashion yearned for the exotic floral shawls imported from northern India, to the dismay of European weavers. Guillaume Ternaux in Rouen found a canny solution: He hired the painter Jean-Baptiste Isabey to design a dozen shawls which were presented to Napoleon, then dutifully worn by Queen Marie Louise and her retinue. Still fashion prevailed; Joséphine de Beauharnais is said to have owned several hundred *indiennes*. The prized originals were woven from the rare fleece of wild Himalayan goats: each spring, wool gatherers collected only the downiest underhair. Cashmeres bridged the gap from personal adornment to interior decoration. During the Second Empire the vast, jewel-hued scarves also served as wall hangings and portieres; they were draped over tables, divans, and pianos. Today's neo–Napoleon III style relies on the same elements to create a stifling yet seductive ambience.

Wool working is a constant in the cultures of all historical eras and geographical areas. Various terms of expression that are still current—fleecing, pulling the wool over someone's eyes, dyed-in-the-wool, going against the wool, woolgathering, much cry and little wool—reveal how closely wool relates to the dynamics of human relations.

It took craftsmen two years to cover the walls of this Parisian dining room in blue felt and to hand-stitch motifs cut from paisley shawls into the fabric.

part 2　　soft *fur*

nishings

"Busy old fool, unruly Sun, Why dost thou thus Through windows, and through curtains call on us? Must to thy motions lovers' seasons run?" John Donne's love poem also reminds us that long before drapes dressed windows, they hung around beds, providing a modicum of domestic warmth and privacy at a time when both of these concepts were in their infancy.

Until the seventeenth century, communal living was the norm in Western Europe: a curtained bedstead represented the only available "room of one's own," for moments of relative solitude or intimacy. Noble lords and their ladies customarily bathed, ate, and slept in drafty medieval halls milling with courtiers and servants, as easily and unself-consciously as the modest burgher sharing bed and board with members of his family and household. At wayside inns—even into the 1800s—perfect strangers were assigned curtained beds in the same chamber. (Contemporary Japanese commuter hotels are a Space Age throwback to such frugal hostelry, with each guest occupying a single-bed-sized cubbyhole, equipped with the basic amenities.)

The vastness of many early beds never fails to awe and amuse,

Bed Hangings

especially in light of their original occupants' very slight stature. The hint of hedonism inherent in the Great Bed of Ware's 10-foot-10-inch-square feet delights today's visitor to Victoria and Albert Museum much as it did almost four hundred years ago when it was new, and a poet surmised that "four couples might cosily lie side by side,/And thus without touching each other abide."

From antiquity, the bed was the most prized possession in the home. The ornamentation of ancient bedcoverings, only suggested by archeological findings, is lavishly described in a second-century A.D. Roman text, according to which coverlets might be delicate, well-woven, shiny, beautifully tinted, flowered, ornate, purple, dark green, scarlet, violet, bordered

with purple, shot through with gold, patterned with animal forms, or scattered with stars.

Until the Renaissance, bed-hanging sets, known as "furniture," were considered more precious—because they were more costly—than the carved wooden frames from which they were suspended. Inventories and wills of this period mentioning colored beds—red, green, purple—refer to the shade of their curtains and coverlets rather than to painted decoration. Catherine de Valois's bedstead in the room known as La Chambre de Ma Dame at Leeds Castle is entirely covered in fabric, according to the prevailing French mode; during the day the curtains were lifted at the corners to form baglike *bourses*. At least 50 yards of fabric might be required to run up adequate hangings

PRECEDING PAGES, LEFT: *A bedroom in Karl Lagerfeld's apartment in Rome, from 1986. The bed is draped in late Louis XVI style, with a fabric by Le Manach. The carpet is of the French Restoration period.*
PRECEDING PAGES, RIGHT: *A crimson silk damask covers the walls and drapes an alcove bed, framed with a tapestry pelmet, in Jacques Garcia's former Paris residence. The cushions are silk, embroidered in red and silver.*

LEFT: *Refurbished in 1793, this bedroom in the manor of Skogaholm in Stockholm is of late Gustavian style: the decor is sparse and the fabrics used for the hangings are simple cottons and linens in traditional Swedish weaves.* ABOVE: *Another simple country bed, in the Marquèze House at the Ecomusée de la Grande Lande in Sabres, France. The original room had no ceiling and the deep canopy was a protection from drafts.*

for a single bed of little consequence, but by the end of the eighteenth century the most elaborate bed sets boasted over three dozen components, including headboard, tester and canopy, inner and outer valances, drapes, *cantonnières* and bonegraces, tiebacks and base.

Perhaps because one third—arguably the most pleasurable third—of one's life is spent in bed, this item is imprinted with something of its owner's status or personality. In the age of kings, a monarch's bed, raised upon a platform, fenced about with a balustrade, or set behind a thicket of columns, commanded the respect of the royal entourage, whether occupied or not. Even the highest echelons bowed or curtsied before the state bed, as churchgoers do before the high altar. Rulers' beds were truly magnificent: Henry II's Florentine consort Catherine de' Medici commissioned black velvet "furniture" richly embroidered with pearls, and it is reported that the master embroiderer Delobel required twelve years to complete state hangings for Louis XIV.

The aura of exclusivity extended even to the space immediately surrounding the bed. The *ruelle*—the "little street" between the bed and the walls—was the celebrated venue for gossip and intrigue with privileged friends; one side was left free while a few chairs were placed on the other for ladies—their escorts stood or, more informally, sat upon the floor. At Versailles, courtiers knew their star was on the rise when the Sun King summoned them to witness at close hand his *petit lever* or *petit coucher*.

According to a 1577 English source, humble

folk might happily bunk down on a straw pallet "with a good round log" as a bolster. An actual sixteenth-century bedstead built of oak, walnut, or beech rated a full complement of mattresses—three, at the very least (which explains the lumpy look of many perfectly reconstituted museum specimens). The bottom palliasse, supported by cords, webbing, or sacking, was also the thickest, stuffed with straw to be changed each spring. Then came an optional number of mattresses containing horsehair, wool, or even moss, which were overlaid by a featherbed. Although this could be replaced by a tick wadded with an inferior grade of cotton, pure swansdown, Bordeaux goosedown, and Antwerp chicken feathers were deemed the most desirable fillings. Personal preference, availability of supplies, and local tradition also affected the composition of the bed: Montaigne opined that "a German made to sleep upon a mattress, an Italian upon a featherbed, and a Frenchman without curtains or fire" would surely fall ill.

A blossoming of beds marked the seventeenth century. Many of the basic upholstered forms evolved then. The so-called French bed, in which all wooden parts were draped, was the simplest; the *lit en housse*—literally, "slipcovered bed"—was a boxlike affair with curtains lifting horizontally in the manner of Roman blinds. Serge, flannel, and linen were generally used to deck these beds. In elegant circles, the vogue was for exceptionally tall and top-heavy confections, with draped, swagged, and tasseled silk hangings, lambrequins crowned with bunches of ostrich plumes, finials in the shape of pineapples and pinecones, torches and floral bouquets, jewel-encrusted insignia, gilt or silvered putti and dolphins. Madame de Maintenon received her friends reclining on a bed 9 feet high, covered in gold and green damask

Writer Paul Duncan's bed in his former home—an eighteenth-century Huguenot house in Spitalfields, London. The massive bed was acquired at an auction sale at a castle in Scotland and decked out in silk, feathers, and tartan by Duncan himself.

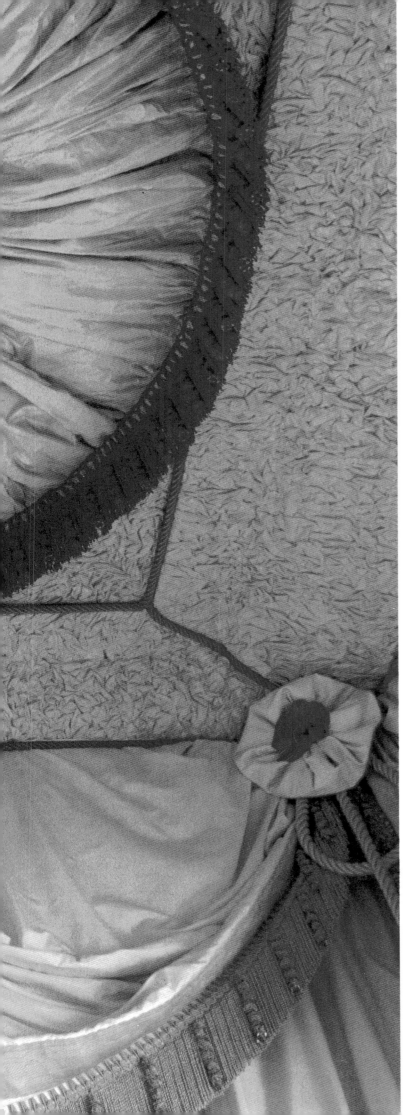

and hung with crimson drapes edged in gold fringe, with tufts of white feathers swaying at each corner. The imperial bed had a domed canopy. A baldachin, unsupported by anterior posts but attached to the wall or ceiling, stretched the full length of the duchess bed, while the angel bed had only a vestigial tester jutting out over the headboard. Understandably, this was an epoch in which gentlemen were admired for their ability to drape an inamorata's bed hangings with elegance.

During the eighteenth century, the traditional duchess canopy was preferred for state beds. Otherwise, informality was the order of the day: sofas and couches displaced unwieldy beds, ensconced in niches, or positioned parallel—rather than perpendicular—to the wall. As cabinetmakers gradually took over bed designing from upholsterers, current events or passing fads prompted new styles which required a more ambitious framework. The airy construction of the *lit à la polonaise,* an homage to Louis XV's wife Queen Maria Leszczynska, was a major innovation. This high-ended bed had a small, central corona resting upon curved posts and surmounted by a sculpted ornament; infinitesimal variations on the same theme characterized the *lit à la dauphine.* The canopied *lit à la turque* had curtains fastened *en culotte de zouave* (with regularly spaced "garters"), reminiscent of bouffant Turkish britches. The Sinomania that swept Europe at this time produced a number of whimsical beds in the Chinese mode, culminating with Thomas Chippendale's sprightly pagoda model. The agreeable economy of the postless Roman bed, with tenting suspended from a decorative wall or ceiling fixture, made it a constant favorite for almost 150 years.

As the century progressed, the upholstery of beds, like their construction, became consider-

LEFT: *The dome of the state bed at Castle Coole in Enniskillen, Northern Ireland, is dressed in the rich splendors of Regency taste—ruched, pleated, and draped silk with rosettes, tassels, and swags which still display the original gold fringes.*

ably less stately. A wider range of fabrics was available, and it became acceptable to use simpler materials, to experiment with unconventional juxtapositions. George Hepplewhite felt that hangings could be fashioned from "almost every stuff which the loom produces"; dimity, chintz, and toiles de Jouy were most appropriate for the bedchamber. Greater attention was devoted to the inner hangings of beds. Ideally, a pleasant sight should gratify the first waking instant—such as the rosetted, ruched, tasseled, and swagged tester on George IV's state bed at Castle Coole in Northern Ireland. Another fine English bed, for example, was "hung with gold and lined with a painted Indian satin." Artisans attempted textile conceits so daring that one critic wondered, "What would Vitruvius think of a dome decorated by a milliner?"

Frills and furbelows were discarded under the Empire. Beds exuded all the *gravitas* of ancient altars or sarcophagi, flanked by crouching griffins and sphinxes, scattered with gilt bronze ornaments. Towering posts in the shape of spears form a military picket around the king's bed in the royal palace at Caserta; the symbolic quiver and torch of Eros overhang the bed of newlyweds.

After about 1825, the iron industry successfully promoted metal frames as durable, hygienic, and versatile. While eliminating the idiosyncratic features of individually commissioned and crafted pieces, mass production—at least initially—did not drastically reduce the variety of available designs. Mid-nineteenth-century advertisements flogged as many as eleven different kinds of beds, from simple camp to more elaborate canopy.

As the bedchamber lost its special status as a reception area, hangings became less ceremonial. Silk was often used to line cotton draperies in soft hues, such as apricot, powder blue, and fawn. Plain muslin curtains, bound or fringed in dark green or red, reflected window treatments in vogue at the time.

Toward the turn of the nineteenth century, a partial victory was claimed by the advocates of uncurtained sleep, including Charles Eastlake, who campaigned against "ponderous curtains which bade fair to stifle [sleepers] before morning." Draperies were also held to be insalubrious havens for dust and bedbugs. Nevertheless, the vogue for canopied beds—whether Arabian, Neo-Gothic, Renaissance Revival, or Old French—has survived intact into our own era. One of the most delightful examples of its longevity is the lofty bedstead in Vittore Carpaccio's painting *Saint Ursula's Dream,* which spawned several copies half a millennium after its execution. The "Saint Ursula bed" inspired various adaptations by architect Sir Edwin Lutyens; Geoffrey Scott had a reproduction made in Italy, now exhibited in the Victoria and Albert Museum; and a third graced the Vanderbilt mansion in New York.

Perhaps the twentieth century's only original addition to the bed department was the ill-fated Age of Aquarius waterbed. (Shiro Kuramata's double bed in which the partners sleep, not side by side, but toe-to-toe deserves dishonorable mention.) Otherwise, it has been an eclectic free-for-all, from Cecil Beaton's Circus Bed vying with the most garish Mediterranean folk Baroque, to the silver bedstead sculpted for Peggy Guggenheim by Alexander Calder, comparable in spirit if not in style to Versailles furniture. Even glamorous bedclothes were first launched by the duchess of Castiglione, whose black, violet, and hot pink sheets scandalized Napoleon III's court. And Mae West's mirrored "so-I-can-see-what-I'm-doing" bed is but a gross reflection of the fanciful looking-glass headboards that were created for Louis XIV and his mistress Madame de Montespan in the Trianon de Porcelaine.

William Constable's 1773 fourposter bed at Burton Constable Hall in Yorkshire was made by Edward of Wakefield and is covered by an elaborate silk damask, trimmed with a passementerie fringe "à jasmins."

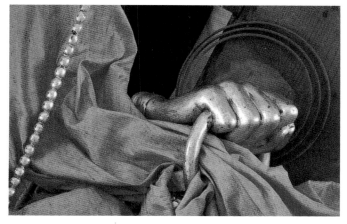

LEFT: *Heavy cut velvet swags divide the first floor reception room from the tiny firelit "retiring room" in Julian Humphrey's former "ordinary" (eighteenth-century restaurant) in Spitalfields, London.* ABOVE: *A silk taffeta by Rubelli slips through a gilded ring and hand tieback by Clare Mosley.*

Rooms, like people, fall into two distinct categories which rarely overlap: day and night. Decorators often ask clients to decide if an area is to be at its best before or after dusk, in order to select fabrics that absorb light or reflect it. There are airy morning rooms into which the sun is intended to stream, only barely filtered through muslin sheers; and then there are richly draped, dressier rooms for entertaining into the night, where artificial light triumphs over the dark. Because electricity can affect the subtlest textural nuances, in interior design the choice of lighting and drapery are inextricably joined. As we anxiously watch the light meter, so did our forebears compute the cost of candles. In *A Complete Body of Architecture* (1756), the architect Isaac Ware noted that, when finishing a room, the expense of lighting should be calculated. By his estimate, a painted room was the least dear, while a "hung" room needed up to ten candles.

Today, cost is still a consideration when upholstering walls. Some designers feel that it is a waste of money, especially for customers with limited budgets: patterns date and fabrics age. Whereas good paintings, furniture, carpets, and objets can always

Drapery

ABOVE: *In Christian Benais's Paris apartment, a white silk blind whose central motif and edge are trimmed with grosgrain has been covered with a transparent protective film, rendering it both rigid and dustproof.* BELOW: *Simple white sheers and a pelmet swag are decorative without being fussy.*

be disposed of at a profit, the resale value of upholstery is nil. Wall hangings are recommended only for those able to recycle the fittings of one home to another. In 1807 the duke of Westminster, "with an eye to economies," borrowed crimson damask off the walls of Eaton Hall in Cheshire to refurbish Grosvenor House in London. The duke of Devonshire in 1922 hung the lobby and china closet of Chatsworth with green brocade from his demolished Piccadilly residence. And until quite recently, Pavia damask from Spencer House in London adorned the Princess of Wales's childhood home in Northamptonshire, Althorp.

Wall hangings gained currency during the Middle Ages. While tapestries guarded chatelains from the cold, drafts, and prying eyes, lesser mortals made do with lengths of linen and worsted, which were suspended from rods or hooks near the ceiling. Tinted, occasionally wood-blocked with a simple geometric pattern, such hangings were changed seasonally. Arundel House wore red and yellow damask during the summer, frieze in the winter months. If fine wall upholstery was not replaced, it was protected from dust and sunlight by loose covers. Hangings were festooned, or "paned"—drawn taut against the wall and bordered with metal fillets, lace, or braid. In paning, strips of different colored cloth—yellow and blue, blue and green, green and red—might be alternated, creating bold contrasts for which the taste, or perhaps the courage, has been lost.

Window curtains made their appearance in the sixteenth century, heralded by a few isolated reports of luxury: Angevin king René's curtains of white bunting edged with blue and gray silk, Anne of Brittany's crimson damask drapes embellished with ribbons. These may in fact have been bed furnishings, since inventories suggest that windows in even the grandest homes were left not only bare but unglazed. Fenestrals, latticed wooden stretchers which could be inserted and removed at will, were commonly used to shield against the weather. Similar frames, screened with oiled buckram, fine linen, or silk taffeta, were known as sun curtains—precursors of today's blinds. In his Paris flat, decorator Christian Benais has given the window shade a modern twist reminiscent of its origins—facing a length of trimmed white silk with transparent plastic film, to stiffen and protect against dust.

At first, curtains were suspended singly from a rod above each window and pulled to one side; eventually, they were paired and drawn to either side of the window. That stock prop of little girls' rooms and embassy salons, the festoon curtain (later dubbed Austrian, or *ballon*), appeared during the seventeenth century. A complicated system of ribbons and rings set along the back of the curtain produced a billowy, swagged effect when it was raised over the window. Elaborate carved pelmets, fabric valances, and lambrequins—sometimes all three together—became necessary to conceal the pulley mechanism.

Countless variations on these basic themes matured during the eighteenth century, particularly in France, the home of home improvements. "Glass curtains" were made of muslin, Italian gauze, and *quinze-seize*. Roman blinds, operating on the principle of festoons, were distinguished by sharper, horizontal folds. Reefed curtains, also called Italian strung, parted in the center by means of a series of widely spaced diagonal cords sewn into the reverse, producing ample, scalloped contours. French drapes curved gracefully back over decorative gilt bronze or passementerie curtain pins. Regularly spaced sets of "garters" gave curtains *à la jarretière* their bouffant line. Drapes with tails, or tapered side panels, frequently associated with Robert Adam's designs, were adopted in Britain and the colonies because they framed window recesses without a drastic reduction of daylight. Often several styles of drapery were combined together in an "everything on it" attempt at sophistication.

RIGHT: *Draw curtains are embellished with a swagged valance ending in tails and trimmed with a fringe.*

Wall treatments too reflected the new softness of life. Painted "chintes," or specially commissioned one-of-a-kind silk damasks, framed by molding, might be featured as the unadorned pièces de résistance of a decor. However, most hangings were intended to serve as a foil for pictures, and single-toned, extravagantly self-patterned fabrics were preferred. (Contrary to popular belief, heavily saturated tints offset Old Masters more forcefully than do neutral shades. Several years ago, it was re-ported that Lee Radziwill's freshly painted white dining room made her collection of English oils "look like nothing"; the successful solution was to do the walls over in crimson.)

In grand establishments, drapes and wall upholstery provided an elementary form of colorcoding. While servants' quarters beneath the eaves were merely whitewashed, cotton prints were used in the family apartments and silk weaves for the reception halls.

Napoleon changed the look not only of nine-

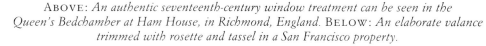

ABOVE: *An authentic seventeenth-century window treatment can be seen in the Queen's Bedchamber at Ham House, in Richmond, England.* BELOW: *An elaborate valance trimmed with rosette and tassel in a San Francisco property.*

teenth-century Europe but of its drawing rooms. The frothy draperies that swathed the Age of Libertinage were brusquely swept aside. The much-admired, and much-frequented, Parisian bedchamber of Juliette Récamier, with its starred cream and azure hangings, conveyed an impression that was at once pleasingly—though not too convincingly—virginal, sepulchral, and imperial. The color schemes of this period, arguably fresher and more pungent than anything up to and including the pastel California style of the 1960s, were based on unprecedented juxtapositions of gold and violet, mint green and lilac, lavender and amber, blue and beige, coral and turquoise. The Roman collector Mario Praz (1896–1982) dreaded replacing the original upholstery of his Empire furniture until he discovered that suitably tinted silks could be ordered from a supplier of ecclesiastical vestments, whose sample books had remained virtually unchanged for two centuries.

ABOVE: *A swagged valance with side tails and a central box pleat, or bell, masks the pelmet board and the head of a peach silk festoon curtain at Barnsley Park in Gloucestershire, England.* BELOW: *An Empire scroll pelmet terminating in an eagle's head at Buscot Park in Oxfordshire, England.*

With its walls
dramatically supporting
tentlike festoons of
simple white fabric, the
bedroom in Mary Goodwin's
London apartment is
a marvelous example of the
inspiration of French
Empire style.

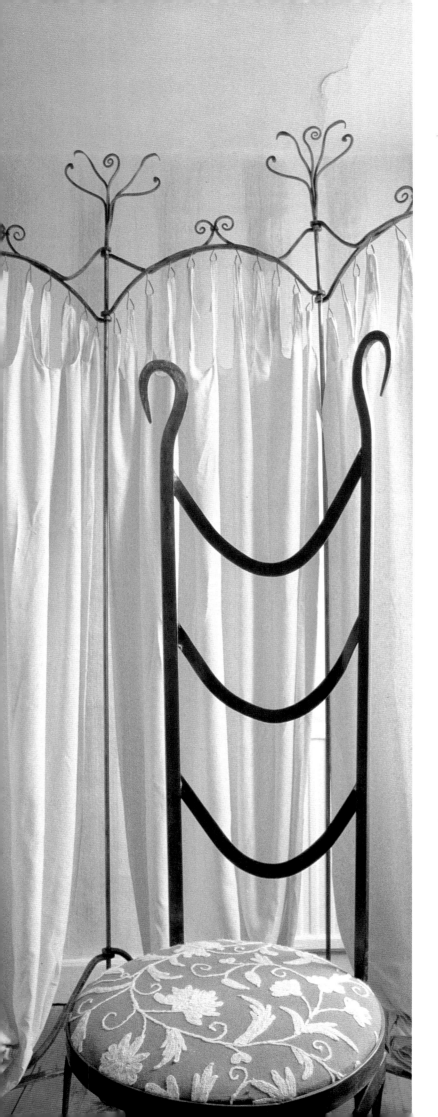

Valances dwindled, and were substituted with rigid curtain headings that rose above the rod to mask it; a number of pleatings—goblet, French, and Flemish—are still in vogue today. Curtains were designed to slide back smoothly on traverse rods without leaving the ground. Fashion prescribed gilt bronze poles or only the narrowest of pelmets, properly adorned. Emblems such as lions', leopards', and rams' heads, as well as the ubiquitous doves and eagles (as at Buscot Park in England) appeared as finials. Antique weapons, especially bows, spears, and javelins, all manner of archeological paraphernalia from urns to mascaroons and thyrsi, were also politically correct: they were thought to exert a stimulating effect on "the fertile imagination."

Military exploits likewise inspired the tent rooms which were all the rage among turn-of-the-century beaux: their walls and ceilings were completely hung with loose or pleated fabric vaguely reminiscent of campaign canopies. The earliest known example, dating to 1777, was executed for the comte d'Artois's residence at Bagatelle on the outskirts of Paris. Eventually, following the example of Josephine, who slept beneath tenting at Malmaison, ladies adopted and adapted the mode, embuing it a suggestive Eastern or Turkish flavor. The Neoclassical architect Karl Friedrich Schinkel designed a white-hung bedroom for Queen Louise of Prussia, and Queen Hortense of Holland fitted her Parisian home with a tented boudoir. As the nineteenth century wore on, totally upholstered rooms lost their aura of exoticism, and were merely referred to as candy- or jewel-box interiors. Renzo Mongiardino's tented sitting room in Palazzo Odescalchi in Rome, upholstered in pink patterned raw Indian silk, marks a recent return to foreign sources.

Under the influence of the Abbé de la Mésangère, and lesser luminaries such as d'Hallevant and George Smith, window treatments developed a quasi-geometrical complexity, requiring up to seven layers of stuff. Sixteen-yard panels of fabric were twisted back and forth, hitched up on cloakpins, secured with rosettes, and bordered with fringe, braid, and bobbles—encasing windows in man-sized cat's cradles more appropriate for a dais than a home. Continuous drapery, uniting two or more windows separated by wall panels, was the upholsterer's tour de force: a textile loop-the-loop suspended, according to one critic, "as if for the purpose of sale or being dried."

After the middle of the nineteenth century, well-dressed rooms discarded these carefully contrived devices, just as a vigorous new industrial order made a shambles of Bonaparte's pristine, well-regulated universe. In this era of bourgeois monarchs, such as Louis-Philippe, Napoleon III, and above all Queen Victoria, many private citizens—the Rothschilds in Britain and France, the Astors, J. P. Morgan, and Isaac Merrit Singer—amassed princely fortunes. The democratization of wealth meant that, while quality in domestic furnishings varied greatly, taste became uniform.

Theatrical, often ill-informed interpretations of styles past or foreign—Oriental, medieval, Renaissance, artist's studio—were embraced enthusiastically. Though Empress Eugénie was mocked for her obsessive revisitations of the Petit Trianon, scorned as "Louis XVI Impératrice," her pastiched elegance was an inspiration to amateur decorators. Cheap wallpaper made fabric hangings a rarity, but every home with a sitting room or at least a front parlor soon sprouted scrolled pelmets and valances. Heavy velvet or chenille curtains puddled on the floor, and netting, lace, or roller blinds screened the windows. Antique paisley scarves and Oriental textiles were used as drapes or tossed over brass rails to serve as portieres.

For the first time, it was fashionable to mix old with new. In *The Europeans*, Henry James describes the decoration of the Baroness Munster's salon: "India shawls suspended, curtain-

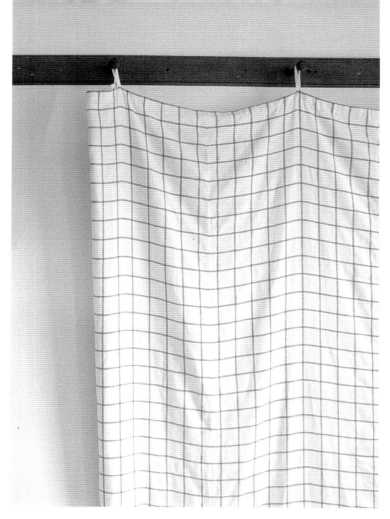

ABOVE: *At the Shaker Village in Pittsfield, Massachusetts, a woven cotton is suspended on simple wooden pegs in one of the sisters' retiring rooms.* BELOW: *An "installation" created by the artist Toni Cordero rests in Fulvio Ferrari's home-cum-gallery in Turin, Italy.*

cented with salmon-pink and tomato cushions and lampshades, was destined to fade. The Gustavian revival, Art Nouveau interiors with their stenciled walls and simple up-and-down drapes, the sober theatricality of Art Deco, all represent different, only apparently contradictory facets of this trend. In the twenties, the Bauhaus slogan "Prototypes for industry," followed by Le Corbusier's chilling definition of houses as "machines for living" and furniture as "equipment," set the tone for this trend: convenience was all.

For years Edith Wharton's belief that the better the house, the less need it had for drapery, was unquestioningly accepted. Indeed, certain windows of outstanding architectural merit, such as the Gothic or the Serlian, should never be dissimulated with drapes. Until recently, floor-to-ceiling pinch-pleated curtains on traverse or motorized rods were the largest concession most people were willing to make to window dressing, even though customized drapery still constitutes the most personal fashion statement available in interior design. Since the 1950s, John Fowler's historically accurate yet imaginative resurrection of early nineteenth-century treatments, particularly in country homes belonging to Britain's National Trust, stimulated several generations of decorators in Europe and the United States to revive lost techniques and to create new accessories. As wall space shrinks and windows expand in contemporary homes, curtains remain the upholsterer's last frontier—and the only remedy to living in glass houses.

wise, in the parlour door"; "anomalous draperies" and "curious fabrics tumbled about in the sitting places"; pink silk blinds and, on the mantel, "a remarkable band of velvet, covered with coarse, dirty-looking lace." At the sight of which the ingenuous Gertrude Wentworth could only admiringly wonder: "What is life, indeed, without curtains?"

A return to basics was inevitable, spearheaded by the Modern movement, whose tenets were best exemplified by the Arts and Crafts Society in England. Its founder, William Morris, preached that houses should be exclusively furnished with "that which you know to be useful and consider to be beautiful."

As modernity became reality for most of the Western world, labor-intensive furnishings in the home were pared down, or even discarded. The aura of the Brighton Room designed in 1911 by Lady Sackville for her daughter Vita, with its blue curtains over yellow sheers, ac-

---

ABOVE LEFT: *Vibrant red curtains hang in an apartment decorated by Jean-Michel Frank in Rome.* RIGHT: *Billowing silk in designer Aldo Cibic's apartment in Venice.*

FOLLOWING PAGES: *Two aspects of an apartment decorated by Agnes Comar in Paris.* LEFT: *The voluptuous swag of heavy curtains in a Fortuny fabric are drawn together on a wall between two windows. The scalloped appliqué work plaid and carpet were also designed by Agnes Comar.* RIGHT: *Silk taffeta curtains are bordered in velvet and trimmed with bells.*

LEFT: *In Renzo Mongiardino's Milan apartment, scraps of antique textiles have been pieced together to form a backdrop for elaborate tassels.* ABOVE: *A chair covered in needlepoint is trimmed with delicate ruching and deep fringe.*

Trim: this brisk, reductive little word hardly does justice to the fanciful exuberance of passementerie. The French term, closer to the Italian *passamaneria,* suggests the marvelous sleight of hand involved in creating the embellishments which are the dressmaker's detail in upholstery. Today's machine-stitched piping, simple braid, or grosgrain ribbon applied to disguise seams bear little relation to the gorgeous galloons, fringes, tassels, and orrises, woven of silk and metallic threads, that enhanced the curve of a pelmet or secured a damask cushion.

Trim—like much of its terminology—is ephemeral, which is why the identification of many items is a matter of conjecture. As one chronicler of Enlightenment mores explained: "There is no product more subject to the inconstancy and caprices of fashion . . . since customers' taste varies without pose"; ribbons, in particular, could be "narrow, wide, patterned, plain, with a right and a wrong side, two right sides, and the most diverse colours and designs according to the talent of the manufacturer, the preferences of the commissioning merchant and fashion itself." Stylish ribbons—*à la coque, au mirliton, à la quadrille, à l'allure*—took their names from current events, personalities, popular songs, and dances. Tassels, often composed of up to six carved and covered

Passementerie

ABOVE: *A detail of the arm of a sofa in Christian Benais's Paris apartment, upholstered in a cotton by Chotard.* BELOW: *Detail of a Louis-Philippe tassel, trimmed with love knots and silk-bound stars.*

ABOVE: *Napoleon III–style tassels sport twisted fringe, jasmins de boules,* diabolos, *and* griffes. BELOW: *Another example of the Napoleon III–style tassel on a silk by Prelle.*

ABOVE: *An example of decorator Renzo Mongiardino's use of rich fabrics and trimmings.* BELOW: *A collection of rosettes, trims, and tassels in Louis XIV and Louis XVI styles.*

ABOVE: *Napoleon III–style tassel with silk trimmed* jasmin de boules *on a silk damask by Prelle.* BELOW: *Gold thread and twisted cord were used for this Napoleon III tieback on a silk damask by Prelle.*

wooden forms, were flat or faceted, dome-, arrow-, ball-, pear-, or screw-shaped. Varieties of fringe included inch, caul, block, campaign, Persian, gimp, vellum, trellis, butterfly, bullion, snailing, tufted, twisted, knotted, netted, fagoted, and swagged. Aside from buttons, bows, and bundles, many diminutive fly ornaments that enliven the trim still clinging to historic pieces remain nameless.

Makers of upholsterers' finery, whose chief virtues were nimble fingers and dry palms, always formed a separate category from the general run of textile workers. Even in Roman times, a sort of plaited decoration was the exclusive specialty of the *cannofori*. In medieval France, *crépiniers* or *dorelotiers* manufactured elaborate borders of silk, wool, or linen for men's and women's headcoverings, liturgical vestments, domestic furnishings, ceremonial trappings, and liveries. Eventually, ribbon weaving and trim making emerged as two distinct branches of the craft. Mid-eighteenth-

century Paris, hub of the fashion world then as now, provided a living for a grand total of 735 *rubaniers* and 530 *passementiers*. No thanks to the Terror and the Industrial Revolution, by the early 1900s Paris numbered seventy ateliers, only a third of which survived the swinging sixties. A handful, such as the Passementerie Nouvelle run by five generations of the Declercq family, still operate today.

Historically, there are two alternating schools of thought regarding trim. The first is that it should stand out sharply. Later, it was considered the height of refinement to match the finishings as exactly as possible.

Fringe was particularly subject to the fluctuations of style. Early documents show that it was used to decorate the finest seats: the throne of Charles VI was fringed with four shades of silk. The seat, arms, back, stretchers, and cushions of the Knole chairs are bedizened with both deep, hanging and narrow, upright crimson silk fringe. Originally, fringe served a pur-

---

ABOVE: *The sofa in this engraving (*"Canapé à la Reine," *from a volume entitled* Le Meuble à l'Epoque de Louis XVI After the Manner of Engravings by Important Masters, De la Fosse, Ranson, Liard, etc.) *is trimmed with swags and tassels and upholstered in an unusual fabric of a trompe l'oeil passementerie design.* RIGHT: *A silk-covered gilt chair and a cream silk tieback at Highclere Castle in Hampshire, England.*

An amazing variety of passementerie accessories from the archives of the Passementerie Nouvelle. These ornamental motifs— flowers, rosettes, and macaroons—were often used to embellish the choux *on draperies, to punctuate festoons, and to trim upholstery.*

pose, as Charles Eastlake pointed out (quoting Augustus Pugin), when it was "nothing more than the threads of silk or wollen stuff knotted together at a ragged edge, to prevent it from unravelling further." During the seventeenth century, a new application for fringe was found —along the edges of bookshelves: each time a volume was removed for consultation, its pages got a summary dusting. Use of fringe dwindled gradually during the course of the eighteenth century, and Napoleon deemed it a "useless" ornament, banishing it from his personal apartments at the Tuileries.

The real glory days came during the Victorian Era, when armchairs, settees, and poufs were skirted with rich, floor-sweeping fringes, self-colored or, better yet, gold. This was the larger-than-life epoch of cords as thick as an elephant's trunk, of rosettes the size of lettuces, of buttons like mushrooms; of social and financial exuberance expressed in every last tasseled tieback and bobbled bellpull.

The Jazz Age penchant for cool, jangling ornamentation (sometimes incorporating raffia, glass, plastic, and wooden beads) was followed by a protracted period of minimalism in passementerie, influenced by less-is-more tendencies in architecture. A renewed interest in "indoorness" and its accessories is the legacy of the last decade's couch potatoes and cocooners, and perhaps—more remotely—of hippiedom's passion for handcrafted macramé and love beads.

Today as in the past, passementerie remains the easiest, least expensive, and most effective way to adorn even the homeliest home.

LEFT: *A variation on the curtain tieback.* RIGHT: *An antique tassel in Jean-Louis Riccardi's Paris home. The three wooden molds would have first been covered with silk, tied, and snailed before the addition of a skirt of mixed colored silks.*

FOLLOWING PAGES, LEFT: *In Jacques Garcia's former Paris house, a Louis XIV armchair is appliquéd with silver motifs of the same period and upholstered in nineteenth-century velvet.* FOLLOWING PAGES, RIGHT: *In Jean-Louis Riccardi's Paris home, floor-sweeping fringes trim a pair of armchairs upholstered in Turkish carpet.*

LEFT: *Unusual swags highlight an armchair in a castle in Vienna, Austria.* ABOVE: *Christian Astuguevieille parcels up a chair with a simple white sheet.*

Upholstery is clothing for houses; it is no coincidence that, in fact as well as fiction, fabrics for furnishing and dress are upon occasion interchangeable. In 1559, sisterly piety prompted Queen Elizabeth I to recycle Edward VI's black velvet robes bordered with damask and Venetian gold, as chair and stool covers. Mary Queen of Scots pressed a cope, chasuble, and several ecclesiastical tunics into service as bed hangings. Conversely, need magnified by vanity inspired the scene in *Gone With the Wind,* where Scarlett converts a set of fringed, moss-green dining-room curtains from Tara into a fetching costume, the better to entrap Captain Rhett Butler. The same basic nonexclusive guidelines that govern fashion also apply to interior design: namely, dressing for the occasion and/or for comfort.

After food, soft furnishings provide the most constant sensory experience in peoples' daily lives: they form the inescapable backdrop to every indoor event. How many memories are triggered, for example, by the anticipatory swoosh of a theater curtain, the damp weight of hastily pressed sheets in cheap Continental hotels, or even the sharp blue sparks flying from fingertips when too

Upholstery

many polyesters come together in a heated office?

The initial impact of an interior is aesthetic, subject to such variables as lighting, scent, and present company. According to personal taste, one may recoil from either the dainty boudoir or the smoke-stained lounge. W. H. Auden wrote that "a living room . . . confronts each visitor with a style, a secular faith; he compares its dogmas with his, and decides he would like to see more of us."

After the initial impact, however, tactile—and therefore textile—values reign supreme. Adjectives such as "warm," "slick," "plush," or "silky" tell as much about the atmosphere as about the textures in a room. It is the touch of things, as much as the look of them, which determines the way we feel about our surroundings. So the choice of upholstery is hardly ever gratuitous. When in 1936 Salvador Dali designed his celebrated sofa modeled after Mae West's still more celebrated lips, he specified the use of bright pink satin, reminiscent of the star's glossy film-studio makeup. Several decades later, American manufacturers issued the piece covered in two shades of pink felt, creating a more up-to-date matte look—and thereby totally subverting the artist's aims.

Upholstery, though the most perishable part of furniture, is meant for body contact, and good upholstery bears the marks of wear proudly. Tradition and common sense dictate that any upholstery intended for seating should incorporate some friction in order to avoid slippage, through the use of pile, a nubby weave, or merely a slightly raised self-pattern. Two hundred years ago, Lady Burlington stated the obvious when she pronounced that "in any velvet that is much used, there will be always the print of people's sitting."

In the seventeenth century, it was customary for fixed fabrics to be replaced but once every several decades. Loose covers, which sometimes included cases to protect gilt legs, were

A well-worn velvet sofa in the handsome double library at Highclere Castle in Hampshire, England.

changed at least twice a year, according to a visitor's relative importance or familiarity.

Although today dry cleaning and spot-resistant finishes have nearly eliminated any need for slipcovers, the custom of temporarily upholstering rooms with lighter fabrics during the summer months has not died out. Slipcovers are no longer intended to fit like gloves: their ample cut and simple bindings display the easy informality of a housedress or pinafore. Christian Astuguevieille's much-imitated draped cases inspired by *furoshiki*, the Japanese art of wrapping, have made the crossover to year-round upholstery. Plastic slipcovers, our era's crackling contribution to the genre, have never proved satisfactory: perspiration outweighs the attractions of transparency.

In the West, utilitarian concerns catalyzed the evolution of the decorative arts. The inhabitants of ancient Greece protected their dwellings from drafts and sunlight with woolen or linen drapes. After Asian trade expanded in the fourth century B.C., they preferred silk hangings. The Romans too had a fondness for what the historian Livy scorned as "foreign luxury," making bedsteads and chairs more comfortable with fine colored stuffs and pillows. Little progress was made during the Middle Ages, when the more fortunate shielded alcoves with curtains or tapestries, and padded stools and hard-backed seats with tie-on squabs.

Upholstery came into its own toward the end of the sixteenth century. The chairs at Knole, Kent, with their velvet-covered arms, legs, and stretchers, introduced the concept of totally upholstered seating. Whimsical contemporary revisitations of this style include Max Cartier's tightly wrapped and string-bound frames and Ruth Harjula's draped, knotted, and swathed pieces—enigmatic, spectral entities.

Eventually seats broke ranks, moving away from the walls and crowding into the center of

LEFT: *In the drawing room of the Von Echstedt manor in Karlstad, Sweden, the walls are decorated with exceptional paintings of biblical scenes, all done on linen. Country Rococo-style chairs are dressed with traditional cotton dust covers to protect the leather seats during the winter months.* ABOVE: *Elements of a suite made in 1778 for the drawing room at Burton Constable Hall in Yorkshire, by the famous English cabinetmaker Thomas Chippendale.*

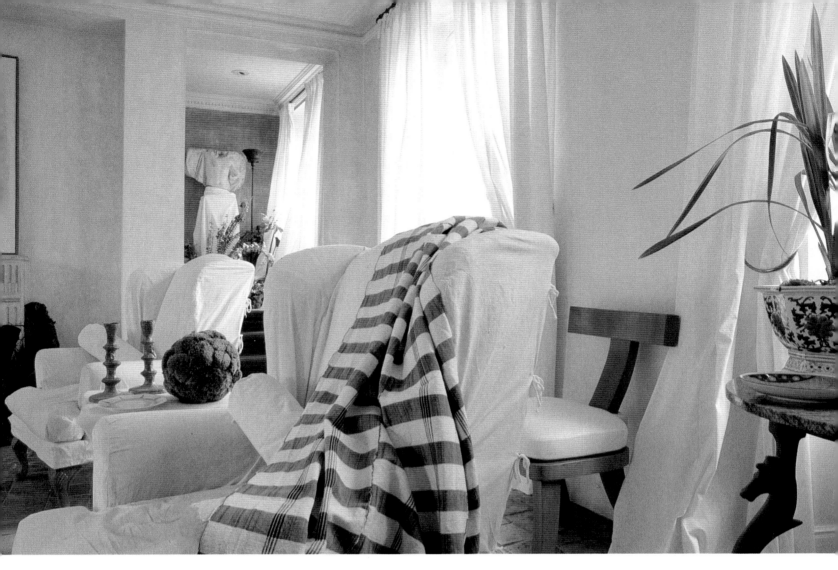

the room, to create the impromptu convivial groupings portrayed in conversation pieces. Freestanding chairs now required upholstering both front and back. The custom of decorating reception halls en suite, with matching furniture, curtains, hangings and accessories, became firmly established: witness the Volury Room at Ham House, hung about 1670 with yellow damask, and Queen Marie Amélie's Fontainebleau apartments, upholstered two centuries later with rose-and-bee-patterned lampas. Private individuals were allowed

greater discretion: Benjamin Franklin provided his wife with two different prints for drapes and chairs, "because these were my fancy."

Much of the basic expertise—stitching and quilting—was borrowed directly from saddlemakers. The upholsterer's craft, thus grounded in the sturdiest techniques available at the time, coupled resilience with resistance. To this day, artisans employ the same simple tools to create custom upholstery: cord, leather thongs, burlap webbing, hammer and nails, springs and pulleys, bosses and pommels. Their

ABOVE LEFT: *In Pascal Morabiti's Parisian office, strips of twine-bound fabric cover the frame of a sofa by French artist Max Cartier.* BELOW LEFT: *Romantic and ghostly, this wildly creative flock of draped, knotted, and swathed chairs surrounding the canopied bed is the work of British artist Ruth Harjula.* ABOVE: *Fresh white cotton loose covers rest on "Queen Anne" chairs designed by Yves-Germain Taralon for his drawing room. A woven cotton coverlet sits in the foreground.*

FOLLOWING PAGES, LEFT: *In the Queen's Closet at Ham House in Richmond, England, the original seventeenth-century hangings of brocaded satin are extremely rare survivals of the most luxurious form of wall decoration of the period. The satin covering the armchair is original, as are the fringe and many of the gilt nails.* FOLLOWING PAGES, RIGHT: *The walls and chairs of the Salon de la Duchesse de Malle of Le Salon Violet in the Musée Condé, in Chantilly, France, are upholstered en suite in an exquisite silver and purple silk.*

special skill is nowhere more evident than in the padding, which is meticulously positioned and molded by hand to suit each individual piece. Although wool, straw, and horsehair were standard, preferences in stuffing varied according to climate or epoch: waste silk, down, and reindeer hair have also served. In the eighteenth century, the English favored a more rounded form of cushioning than was popular on the Continent, achieved with two layers of wadding instead of one. The unmistakable extra springiness typical of Victorian furniture comes from a strip of cotton wool between the cloth covering and the padding.

The only, albeit revolutionary, innovation in upholstery introduced after 1700 (except for the manmade filling products adopted in our century) was the spring. A few feeble attempts were made in France during the third quarter of the eighteenth century to fabricate a *bergère à ressorts*, but it was not until the 1820s that the now ubiquitous springed armchair was patented across the Channel.

As craftsmen became more versatile, they turned their attention to the embellishment of upholstery—and soon realized that the luxury differential empowered them to set their own price. It is difficult to imagine spending over three times as much for bedclothes as for a lot of Raphael drawings. Yet Charles I of England did this in 1651, when he forked out £1,000 for an embroidered green satin spread and hangings, only two decades after he had acquired the seven tapestry cartoons of the Acts of the Apostles by the Italian master.

Taking their cue from contemporary women's dress, upholsterers replaced the sobriety of a piecrust ruffle or a flat, profiled valance with the virtuoso effects of ruching, flouncing, swagging, choux, furbelows, and festoons. They copied the draped simplicity of Neoclassi-

The fabric of an eighteenth-century silk cope is used to upholster a meridienne especially designed by Jacques Garcia. The gold braids are eighteenth-century; the tassels and silk fringes were copied by Passementerie Nouvelle from archive designs.

PRECEDING PAGES: *Eighteenth-century chairs with upholstered seats at Mount Vernon.*

....

ABOVE: *Three engravings of daybeds taken from* Le Meuble à l'Epoque de Louis XVI After the Manner of Engravings by Important Masters De la Fosse, Ranson, Liard, etc. RIGHT: *The deep-buttoned interior of the gala carriage built for the president of the Republic, ca. 1895, is of silk satin.*

cal fashion, and mirrored the busty, bustled silhouettes of the second half of the nineteenth century. In every era the names of queens and royal favorites—Pompadour, Josephine, Eugénie, Victoria—evoked grand interiors.

Even the names of chairs paid backhanded tribute to supposedly quintessential feminine virtues and failings. The *caquetoire*—a low chatterer's seat—appeared in the seventeenth century, followed by languorous *veilleuse* daybeds, fireside *chauffeuses,* and a bevy of *voyeuses* with padded back rails for eavesdroppers' elbows. The nobler seats included *duchesses* and *marquises,* with their exotic reclining *ottomane* and *sultane* sisters. Under the Second Empire, loveseats ranged from the innocent, all-talk-and-no-action *causeuse* or *confident* to the more promising *amorino*. The *indiscret* had, predictably, three seats. The *fauteuil de l'amour,* created for a turn-of-the-century Parisian brothel, positioned the pair of users head-over-heels. Another chair built for male convenience, designed by architect Eugène Viollet-le-Duc, featured a special back for men's tailcoats.

While a few hard-line censors scoffed at the "petticoats" and "millinery," which they felt degraded the decorative arts, rapture at the resultant medley of female and furniture was doubtless the reaction of the average man-about-town. Agog with prefeminist sentiment, Théophile Gautier wondered: "What could be more enchanting than a group of women, of different and contrasting beauty, sitting on a pouf at the center of a salon, amidst an eddy of guipures and lace which foams at their feet like the sea beneath the feet of Venus?"

Deep buttoning deserves special mention in the category of ornamental anthropomorphism. One scholar, who described *le style capitonné* as umbilical dimples, saw it as a sublimation of the most bourgeois part of the body, the belly. This upholstering device evolved from the earlier float tufting. Tufts consisted of small bunches of silk fibers tightly bound around the middle with a linen thread, which was passed through the upholstery and helped hold the

Jeanne Lanvin's boudoir in
Paris, which was designed
by Armand Rateau
in 1921–22, is replicated
in this exhibit
at the Musée des Arts
Décoratifs in Paris.

padding firmly in place. Although buttoning is believed to have been first incorporated by Robert Adam in a chair design of about 1780, its heyday arrived some fifty years later. After the middle of the century, the habitat was awash in buttons on settees, footstools, frames, and walls. In humble spheres, because such upholstery did not wear well and therefore required frequent replacement, cast-off gowns were commonly used to cover buttoned furniture. Their solid colors and small prints could not be deformed by its swells and furrows.

The finest hour of *capitonnage* came in 1878, when the Paris Exposition Universelle featured a completely buttoned *salon de repos,* done up in a soothing combination of peacock blue and pink silk. Buttoning was often employed in the most luxurious railway coaches, where it served a purpose in cushioning against jolts; see Napoleon III's deep green silk *wagon-salon.*

Today, dimpled furniture looms large in the decors of professional fans of Second Empire trappings—Henri Samuel, whose name is closely associated with the Rothschilds, as well as the American designer Robert Denning. In Paris, Yves Marthelot molds Baroque poufs and settees from extravagantly trimmed fabric coils.

Due to the inexorable swing of style's pendulum between the rectilinear and the serpentine, certain motifs in upholstery emerge as perennials. Floral compositions have always been in good odor, from the Italian Renaissance thistle to Rococo bloom-laden meandering vines, from Queen Victoria's demure rosebud chintz to France's turn-of-the-century "enraged poppies" and "liliaceous exquisitenesses." Today's infatuation with all things British means that conventional flower prints are now more popular than they have ever been during the past fifty years. Curtains and slipcovers be-

strewn with blowsy, patinated cabbage roses are universally recognized as the signature trademark of the London firm of Colefax & Fowler—or one of their transatlantic competitors, such as Mark Hampton or Parish Hadley.

Geometrics—stripes, checks, dots—are the alternative. Because geometrics lack the obvious panache and variety of florals, their range of effect is often sorely misjudged. According to a persistent medieval superstition, striped materials—worn by lepers, prostitutes, and every sort of sinner—were the devil's own stuff. This taboo vanished with the introduction of mechanized weaving which resulted in irresistibly cheap, simply patterned textiles. Since the design cannot get lost or distorted among folds, stripes are a sensible choice in furnishing. A rule to remember, however, is that horizontals broaden; verticals heighten.

Employed daringly, geometrics can achieve a stylish, even dramatic look. The halls of Balmoral Castle, hung with Royal and Dress Stewart tartan by Thomas Grieve in 1853, illustrate the pageantry of Scotomania at its most fulsome. Exotic leopard-spotted designs originally came into vogue during the 1790s, and are now enjoying—with textile artist Manuel Canovas, among others—a further burst of popularity.

"Sitting pretty," "the lap of luxury," and other colloquialisms show how closely we associate upholstery with well-being. Today we have the choice between the mature appeal of Ron Arad's bosomy *No Spring Chicken* and the brittle charms of Madonna as rendered in the black-corseted *Bra Chair* by Tev Vaughn. For those who find solace in food, MacLeod's *Sushi* chair and pouf hit the spot. The master of soft art Claes Oldenburg once suggested that the need of love translates into the desire for a soft world—that is, a world with give.

CLOCKWISE FROM ABOVE LEFT: *Two details of the Baron and Baroness Rothschild's apartment taken in 1984 reveal the armorial, allegorical, and Italian Renaissance dishes which hang above the deep-buttoned sofa in the salon and a chair upholstered in a floral tapestry in the Baroness's bedroom. The curious intertwined shapes of an armchair form part of an extraordinary collection of beautiful and bizarre pieces to be found in antique collector Mony Linz Einstein's apartment and gallery in Paris. A cotton damask was used for the armchair upholstery in Tricia Guild's London house.*

part 3
a creative

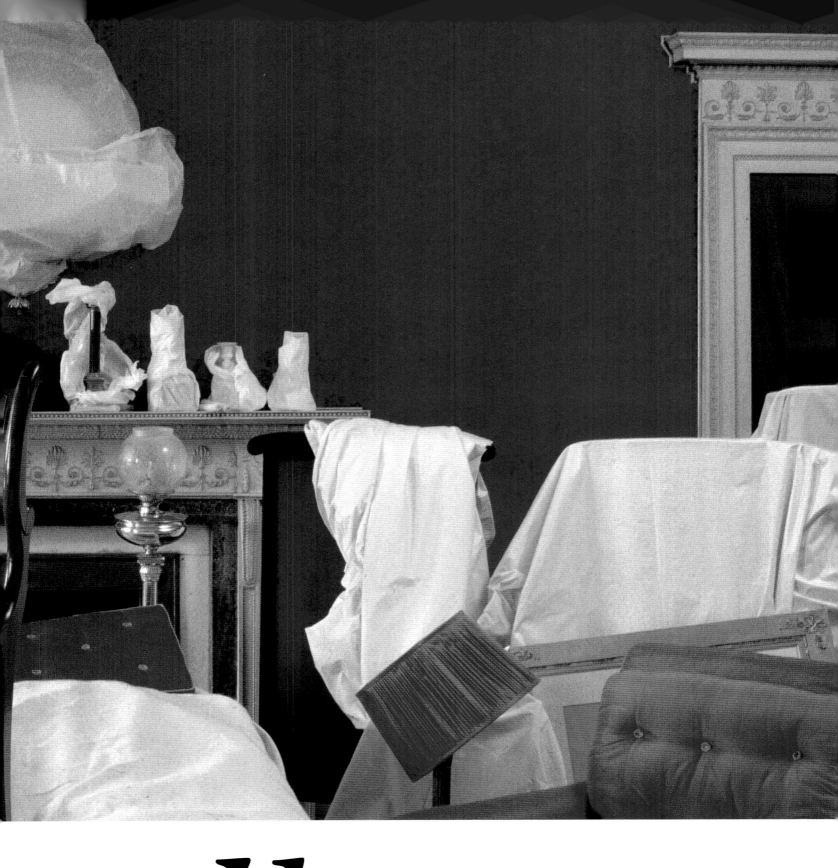

album

PRECEDING PAGES: *Furniture and a mirror are swathed in protective dust sheets during the restoration of the state bedroom in Castle Coole in Enniskillen, Northern Ireland.*

....

LEFT: *A chair in the Alexandrian Cottage on the edge of the park at Peterhof in Petrodvorets, Russia.* ABOVE: *Architect/ decorators Patrick Naggar and Dominique Lachevsky hang a simple striped fabric in the stairwell of an art collector's Swiss home.*

Eclecticism is the best term for today's style of decoration. According to taste and clientele, most interior designers have adopted a position midway between those of the museum curator and the gentrified ragpicker. The glittering prizes they acquire in the salesrooms of London and New York are offset by rare —or merely quaint—objets trouvés from local flea markets.

It is the manner in which fabrics are employed in an interior that reveals the designer's and the proprietor's intent. The muslin dustcover that balloons around the mirror in the state bedroom at Castle Coole signals curatorial concern, or perhaps just good housekeeping. Curtained banisters protect children—and pets—from a tight spot or a fall; thick fabric covers protect a precious book; pillows of every size and form cradle the anatomy—these illustrate the fastidious yet imaginative ways in which cloth translates consideration.

The "upholder" was the decorator's predecessor, and until the seventeenth century his status was relatively undistinguished. The Hampton Court records show that he operated as a purveyor of goods, "making the Chaires and fire screene and finding all mate-

Decoration

rials as feathers, nailes, Tacks, dyed Lynnen, Silk Thread, Girth Webb." Eventually, however, the upholsterer acquired greater importance than the cabinetmaker (relegated to the confines of the servants' hall) whose handiwork provided the support for his flourishes. Soon he was vying with the architect for the ear of the patron—or the patroness, whom he was perilously "versed in ways of leading."

Distrustful critics accused the upholsterer of being "Frenchified," which implied then exactly what it does today in English-speaking lands. He "was originally a species of Taylor," the *London Tradesman* observed loftily in 1747, "but by degrees has crept over his Head, and set up as a Connoisseur in every article that belongs to a House." As a general contractor, he employed "journeymen in his own proper calling, cabinet makers, glass-grinders, looking-glass framers, carvers for chairs, Testers and Posts for Beds, the Woolen Draper, the mercer, the Linen Draper and several species of smiths and a vast army of tradesmen and other mechanic branches."

The divulgation of style took place through personal contacts, on an individual rather than an institutional basis—although often the distinction was moot. The Sun King's residences, together with those of his chief courtiers, were treated and regarded as showrooms for the nation's arts. Throughout Europe, as the Grand Tour emerged as the rite of passage for gentlemen of breeding and culture, access to most great houses was readily granted to properly introduced, "respectable" parties. Letters home reported in graphic detail all manner of foreign novelties, down to the last burnished keyhole.

Scholarly publications also encouraged the spread of fashion. The birth of Neoclassicism was sparked by the engravings illustrating the archeological discoveries at Pompeii and Herculaneum in 1748. Pattern books by Thomas Chippendale, Robert Adam, and Thomas Sher-

aton sustained the vogue for the next fifty years. Recurrent bouts of "Grecian Taste and Roman Spirit," manifest in the Empire, Regency, and Federal styles, may be ascribed to the vast popularity of picture albums by Thomas Hope, and by Charles Percier and Pierre François Léonard Fontaine, Bonaparte's builders.

Periodicals were legion, surprisingly more so than in the present era of widespread literacy. In the United States alone there were approximately a half million titles during the early decades of the nineteenth century. In Britain *The Repository of the Arts* acquired a substantial readership, and the Weimar *Journal für Literatur, Kunst, Luxus und Mode,* with its potpourri of frivolous and educational topics, was the ancestor of today's lifestyle magazines. Oddly enough, the internationally recognized arbiter in matters of taste was a man of the cloth, Abbé Pierre de la Mésangère. His *Meubles et Objets de Goût* chronicled the evolution of taste between 1802 and 1835.

During the second half of the century, interior decoration captured the attention of the literati as a subject of artistic, philosophical, even political significance. Edmond de Goncourt wrote about *La Maison de L'Artiste;* Harriet Beecher Stowe coauthored *The American Woman's Home* with her sister; Edgar Allan Poe elaborated a *Philosophy of Furniture.* Edith Wharton, who together with Ogden Codman published *The Decoration of Houses,* pronounced deal furniture and dimity curtains "more beautiful, more logical and more harmonious" than the most gilded of palaces. Outraged cries of dissent rose from the opposing camp, led by the decadent Italian aesthete Gabriele d'Annunzio and the Sitwell siblings, with their flamboyant, make-believe medievalism.

The immediate commercial response to these totalitarian aesthetic systems was the department store, stocked with an array of distinctive items for the well-appointed home. Samuel

RIGHT: *Two unusual hotel lobby seats are placed on either side of the fireplace in Christian Benais's drawing room. The upholstery, curtains, and cushions are in a fabric Benais designed for Chotard.*

The magnificent entrance
hall in Jacques Garcia's
former house in the Marais
quarter of Paris. The blue
hangings and the undercloth
on the central table were
rescued from the fire that
destroyed the Tuileries
palace in 1871. The stools
are covered in silk velvet
with gilt passementerie.

Bing's establishment in Paris, but most especially Sir Arthur Lazenby Liberty's vast oak-beamed emporium on Regent Street, were prototypes for the comprehensive services and standardized lines of merchandise today provided by Laura Ashley, Ralph Lauren, Conran's, Habitat, and Ikea.

Just as the business of decoration began to evolve into a serious money-making proposition, the role of the designer became more akin to that of the classless artiste. The interior decorator was acknowledged as a protagonist rather than a stage hand in the theater of life. It was a society lady, Syrie Maugham, who in the 1930s introduced the all-white interior. Until this time, white had been primarily associated with tropical furnishings and sanitary fittings; muslin-tented Neoclassical chambers were also a distant source. Imitated by Maugham's American colleague Elsie de Wolfe, the white-draped interior survived through the 1940s,

and can still be admired in countless Hollywood movie sets. A refrigerated version re-emerged some twenty years ago, when twin white sofas set around a white coffee table, against a backdrop of white walls, were the cardinal elements of minimalist Italian design.

The versatile Elsie de Wolfe also synthesized what Le Corbusier mocked as the "Louis A, B, and C" styles into a heterogeneous Old French look, with which she refurbished not only the Trianon at Versailles, but also Henry Clay Frick's Fifth Avenue mansion. Madeleine Castaing, whose maverick brand of eclecticism was at first slow to travel beyond her Rue Jacob premises, was perhaps the last of the great tastemakers.

The current generation of European *créateurs*, including Andrée Putman and Ettore Sottsass, Jean-Michel Wilmotte, and Philippe Starck, have adopted the vigorous approach of the master *ensembliers* of the Art Deco period, such

ABOVE: *In decorator Frederic Méchiche's Paris gallery, an all-white atmosphere prevails. The antique sofa of the Louis XIV period is covered in simple white cotton toile. The frames of the "Lysis" chair, designed by Méchiche, are painted white to simulate plaster.* RIGHT AND FOLLOWING PAGES: *The epitome of the famous Jacques Grange style is depicted beautifully in two views of his own apartment in Paris overlooking the Palais Royal—once the home of the great French novelist Colette.*

as Emile Jacques Ruhlmann and Eileen Gray. Their knowledge of the principles of cabinetmaking and architecture, combining traditional craftsmanship with industrial techniques, has enabled them to construct objects subtly calibrated to their surroundings.

Christian Benais has a passion for soft furnishings, preferably antique. He scours flea markets and fairs for silks, printed toiles, and remnants of passementerie to cover the multiform, ubiquitous cushions which are his trademark. Benais also designs his own patterns, copied after styles of the past. He favors a spectacular display of rich and exotic stuffs, which he presses into service as tablecloths, swagged portieres, or drapes. In re-creating the ambience of yesteryear, Benais even stocks clients' homes with impeccable old linens.

Jacques Garcia is attracted to objects and places with strong historical associations. A showcase for his Baroque style is his former Parisian home, which once belonged to the Sun King's architect Jules Hardouin-Mansart, who completed Versailles and built Place Vendôme and the Grand Trianon. The piano nobile was a treasury gorged with mementos from the Grand Siècle and the equally grand centuries immediately before and after. The blue hangings in the entrance hall were rescued from the fire that destroyed the Tuileries Palace in 1871. In his principal salon a chair from Versailles, originally covered with silver leaf, was upholstered in nineteenth-century silk velvet. The duchess de Mouchy, Marie-Antoinette's lady-in-waiting, slept in the bedroom where a Jacob *lit à la polonaise* was draped in green taffeta, lined with ivory silk, and trimmed with gilt passementerie and old rose fringe.

Jacques Grange is the most quintessentially French of contemporary designers. He has created interiors for unofficial ambassadors of French style such as Yves Saint-Laurent, Catherine Deneuve, and Isabelle Adjani. A Grange room is imbued with a serene and studied classicism—although he is often accused of taking refuge in the safe tones of beige and cream. Grange's association with major tastemaking antiques dealers, such as Didier Aaron, has given him a connoisseur's approach to art, allowing him to combine contemporary and traditional design with a soupçon of wit.

Renzo Mongiardino is designer by appointment to industrial princes such as Heinrich Thyssen and Gianni Agnelli. His distinctive cinematographic palazzo style is based on a rich pastiche of traditional crafts. Based in Milan, Mongiardino employs a stable of artisans working exclusively for him, to create a total environment in which every surface is hand-worked, -tinted, and -textured. The Paris residence of an illustrious Italian family is evocative of Luchino Visconti's masterworks: the theatrical effect of trompe-l'oeil paneling, painted wooden furniture, and marbling is magnified by the use of specially dyed and stamped velvet hangings and cushions with embroidered and jeweled appliqués, suggesting some bygone aristocratic epoch.

Elisabeth Garouste and Mattia Bonetti, the current darlings of Gallic design, are closely associated with Christian Lacroix's giddy fashions. Their extravagant "neobarbarian" furniture is reminiscent of, if not exactly inspired by, nature: the duo's mossy couch and gilt twig chairs have become classics. With a broad humor rare in French design, Garouste and Bonetti pay tribute to Bernard Picasso's passion for music, by covering Louis XVI chairs and sofa with white linen trimmed with black braid and leather appliqués in the shape of notes.

RIGHT: *Decorator Renzo Mongiardino used antique fabrics to cover the sofa cushions in the anteroom of a seventeenth-century town house in Paris.*

FOLLOWING PAGES: *In Bernard Picasso's seventeenth-century chateau, Elisabeth Garouste and Mattia Bonetti have covered Louis XVI chairs and sofa with off-white linen braided in black and scattered with appliquéd leather instruments and musical notes.*

LEFT: *Trompe l'oeil William Morris–style chairs painted by Japanese artist Hisachika Takahashi recovered in Melbury, Ludlow, Honeysuckle, and Trent fabrics, which were designed by or adapted from William Morris designs. Block-printed at the time of Morris & Co., they are today manufactured and marketed by Liberty of London.* ABOVE: *At Charleston Farmhouse in Sussex, curtain and pelmet are done in the original "Grapes" fabric, designed by Duncan Grant in 1937.*

As decorators attempt to invent instant history, textile designers have been encouraged to create contemporary memorabilia of their own.

William Morris's message to the modern age, inherent in the rich handmade stuffs of the Arts and Crafts movement, was a warning against the excesses of industrialization, against sacrificing idiosyncratic beauty to mere technological perfection. In Britain his call was taken up in a bohemian key by the short-lived Omega Workshops, founded in 1913 by the art historian Roger Fry. A Bloomsbury fixture for six short years, the atelier exhibited household objects—lampshades, screens, curtains, furniture—created by Postimpressionist stylists and artists such as Vanessa Bell and Duncan Grant. The decoration of the couple's Sussex home, Charleston (now a museum), displays a playful, kaleidoscopic exuberance. (A number of the original fabric designs —such as Wind, Grapes, and Urn—have been reproduced by Laura Ashley.) While Fry defended "the expressive quality" of their work, critics not infrequently or unjustly accused Omega artisans of slaphappy execution.

Textile Design

CLOCKWISE FROM ABOVE: *Duncan Grant and
Vanessa Bell's studio at Charleston farmhouse in Sussex,
England. Three fabrics reproduced by Laura Ashley—
White, Wind, and Urn—shroud the chairs in front of the
fireplace decorated by Duncan Grant. An armchair
in the library is upholstered in Clouds, a 1932 design by
Duncan Grant for Allan Walton Ltd. and reproduced
by Laura Ashley in 1987. Vanessa Bell did the artwork on
the book jackets. In Vanessa Bell's bedroom, two chairs
are upholstered in Grapes, a 1937 design by Duncan Grant.
The screen, decorated by Duncan Grant in 1913,
is an early example of the Omega workshop productions.
Reproductions of Grant and Bell's fabrics decorate
Nick Ashley's London home. In Clive Bell's bedroom at
Charleston, White fabric, designed by Vanessa Bell
in 1913, covers the cushions of an armchair. The corner
cupboard was decorated by Duncan Grant.*

During the twentieth century, decorative abstraction spilled over into fabrics from modern art. Studied spontaneity was the stock in trade of the School of Paris painters. Of highly divergent aesthetic tendencies, their names were also linked to avant-garde theater and fashion design. In the 1920s, Ukrainian-born Sonia Delaunay established an *atelier simultané* where she produced "simultaneous fabrics" noted for their brilliant chromatic harmonies and contrasts. Their finely calibrated patterns, originally inspired by the quilts pieced together from scraps by the Russian peasants of Delaunay's youth, were also reminiscent of Cubist art.

A colorist like Delaunay, Raoul Dufy also wielded the talents of a master draftsman. His vibrant sketches of quintessentially Parisian festivities, amusements, and landmarks—races, promenades in the Bois de Boulogne, the Eiffel Tower—still inform our vision of Gallic gaiety. Stylist Paul Poiret, the Bianchini-Férier firm in Lyons, and the American Onondaga Company all employed Dufy as a textile designer through the 1930s: his sense of line and shade as well as his knowledge of engraving technique enabled Dufy to invent memorable patterns. As an artist he was careful to skirt the major manufacturing pitfalls of repetitiousness and excessive polish. Dufy often retouched designs with a special oiled plate, which gave the impression of accidental manual irregularities.

Even the iconoclastic Pablo Picasso did not turn down special commissions from the dean of Art Deco designers, Jean-Michel Frank. His 1951 dove design for the international youth and students' peace festival in Berlin was the artist's last and—perhaps most meaningful—contribution to the textile arts. The painter Graham Sutherland too became briefly involved in fabric design in Britain. During the 1950s

....

ABOVE FAR LEFT: *Designs on cotton by Sonia Delaunay for Bianchini Férier.* ABOVE LEFT: *A design by Pablo Picasso for the Festival Mondial de la Jeunesse et des Etudiants pour la Paix, Berlin 1951.* BELOW LEFT: *"Deauville," a printed cotton designed by Raoul Dufy.* RIGHT: *Another Dufy design, also for Bianchini Férier.*

the best-selling items in Britain were reproduced after traditional French prints. The British Ministry of Works ordered yards of the
1958 Abstraction to upholster public installa-
tions throughout the country.

A welcome element of surreal whimsy
emerged in Italy at this time, with Piero Fornasetti's graphic patterns. A Milanese print-
maker, Fornasetti worked closely with the
metaphysical painter Giorgio de Chirico and
his brother Alberto Savinio. Fornasetti's fascination with and mastery of the engraved image
informed his own original designs, which he
applied not only to textiles but to an array of
useful and/or ornamental objects. Their somber precision, foiled by droll juxtapositions,
skewed foci, and trompe l'oeil, is reminiscent
of Max Ernst's haunting Surrealist collages.

Sue Timney and Grahame Fowler in London
have revived the Neoclassical elegance of the
toile peinte. Their stylized designs are often inspired by architectural motifs from historic
pattern books; their sense of fun is almost For-
nasettian. In addition to textiles, Timney and
Fowler prints have been successfully adapted to
such diverse household accessories as wallpaper,
ceramics, carpets, and stationery. In the couple's Victorian family home, distinctive Timney and Fowler graphics accent a heterogeneous
jumble of wrought-iron, Arts and Crafts wood-
work, Japanese porcelain—and 1950s junk.

The British designer Carolyn Quartermaine
is principally a colorist: her fauteuils for the
French bicentennial, upholstered in red, white,
and blue silk, make their point without words.
She spells out her message, however, in brilliantly hued screen prints, which reproduce
enlarged script from eighteenth-century manuscripts. In a daring revival of medieval paning,

LEFT: *"Fruit Cup," a screen-printed chintz produced
by the Libert studio in Paris in 1953.* ABOVE RIGHT: *A
selection of Fornasetti's architectural fancies printed
in cotton.* ABOVE FAR RIGHT: *A 1940s wrought-iron chair
appropriately bedecked in a wrought-iron print by
Timney Fowler.* BELOW RIGHT: *More Timney Fowler
prints which have been skillfully mixed with Fornasetti
pieces and their own carpet and ceramics designs.*

ABOVE LEFT: *London-based designer Carolyn Quartermaine screen-prints fragments of French eighteenth-century manuscripts in gold textile pigment onto a variety of stunningly colored Chinese silks.* BELOW LEFT: *British textile designer Nigel Atkinson's "Bamboo Pleat" in latex and silk is used to cover the cushions on this astonishing bronze bed by sculptor Edward Cronshaw. The bedspread and fabric in the foreground are sculptured velvets also by Atkinson.* ABOVE: *Two hand-painted fabrics fringed with natural twine by Eliakim.* LEFT: *A polyester pebble weave fabric by Eliakim is scattered with boot buttons, twig bundles bound with silver twine, hand-painted felt, and resin coquilles dipped in gold.*

she alternates lengths of silk with gilt paper strips. Her particular flair for soft furnishings comes from Quartermaine's traditional, hands-on attitude to decoration: she belongs to that almost extinct breed of designer-upholsterers.

Another Briton, Nigel Atkinson, has created revolutionary textile hybrids that are as effective on stage as in the hands of avant-garde stylists such as Issey Miyake, Missoni, and Azzedine Alaïa. These state-of-the-art fabrics, often displayed in galleries, can create startling sculptural foci in interior design. Latex combined with silk gives Bamboo Pleat (used here to shape an array of twisted cushions) a bizarre life of its own. Like Atkinson, the versatile Eliakim was celebrated for his one-of-a-kind hand-painted hangings, and retained a crafts-

man's approach to industrial production. Mixed media give his stuffs an eye-catching variegated finish. Eliakim's polyester pebble-weave is extravagantly embellished with golden resin coquilles, boot buttons, bundles of twigs bound with silver twine, and colored felt.

Four women—Christelle Le Dean, Blandine Lelong, Isabelle Rodier, and Corinne Hellein —together form Robert Le Héros, a young French textile firm. It specializes in bold, historically evocative patterns, featuring mythological figures and symbols. The fabrics carry almost untranslatable titles that sound like lines from Dada poetry: Coup de pied à la lune (Kicking the Moon), Saut de l'ange (Angel's Leap), Ton bonhomme qui tombe (Your Guy's Falling), Que tout ceci reste entre nous (Be-

ABOVE: *Oilcloth on a linen backing printed with Breton seafaring images by Robert Le Héros.*
RIGHT: *Two prints by British textile designers Kim Bentley and Sally Spens.*

FOLLOWING PAGES, LEFT: *A velvet panel by Norélène. The velvets and cottons of this textile design firm are first hand-dyed, then block-printed, principally with geometric motifs, immediately bringing to mind patterns of Venetian pavements.* FOLLOWING PAGES, ABOVE RIGHT: *A collection of shimmering silks from the "Silk Road" collection designed by the master designer/weaver Jack Lenor Larsen.* FOLLOWING PAGES, BELOW RIGHT: *Woven textile samples by Brussels-based designer Anne Beetz, who is known for her personal and original colors and for her exploration of new weaving technologies.*

tween You and Me). Robert Le Héros fabrics—often limited editions or special commissions—are printed in a rich though narrow range of natural, earthy tones, on rough unbleached linens and cottons. Another ecologically correct team effort is that of Kim Bentley and Sally Spens in London. They met at art school and successfully market their handcrafted fabrics. Bentley and Spens's spontaneous calligraphic patterns, boldly splashed with color, hark back to the heyday of the Omega atelier.

The sumptuous moiré silk velvets of Norelene are also the result of collaboration. Mother and daughter Hélène and Nora Ferruzzi live and work in Venice. Although collectors compare their delicately calibrated, painterly geometrics to Paul Klee's gouaches, Norelene designs reflect the watery views of La Serenissima as well as the city's art: the mosaic palazzo facades, the wavy tessellated floors of San Marco. Nubby wild silk was the Ferruzzis' first love, hand-dyed, then wood-blocked; now they decorate cotton, linen, and even leather. Norelene fabrics show to best advantage when used as drapes or wall hangings; as upholstery, they should never be cut, stitched, and ruched, but flung opulently over a divan.

For several decades Jack Lenor Larsen has been recognized as the dean of American textile designers. Deemed by some critics to err on the conservative side, Larsen is nonetheless admired for his stylish abstractions which blend handsomely with modern architecture and furniture of the spare, "less-is-more" school. His patterns never overwhelm, but form a neutral though subtly textured background for people as well as objects. Larsen's familiarity with advances in industrial weaving and printing technology has enabled him to achieve novel visual effects while increasing durability. He is one of the foremost specialists on using natural and synthetic mixes in office interiors and public spaces to enhance the effects of lighting, air-condi-

tioning, and soundproofing. Larsen is understandably a favorite with corporate patrons.

Anne Beetz, working in Brussels, produces sober yet subtle weaves in wool, silk, and cotton, occasionally highlighted with Lurex thread. Born of considerable hi-tech experimentation, Beetz's discreet linear patterns—checks, stripes, houndstooth—have a timeless yet distinctly contemporary flavor. They make the ideal complement to modern settings, as screens, wall coverings, and partitions.

Francis Miller and Patrick Bertaux are a pair of French designer-decorators who look beyond national heritage for inspiration. Compulsive travelers both, they scour Morocco, Egypt, and Australia for ethnic pieces with the muted tones, naïf patterns, and pared-down shapes that distinguish the Miller and Bertaux style. Though rarely executed in precious materials, their furniture and textiles achieve a formal sophistication that transcends mere craftsmanship. Their exploration of the Orient in particular has taught Miller and Bertaux that decorating is simply a question of "knowing how to place objects in a certain manner."

The ultimate unconstrained and untrained designs come from the hands of babes. Ever since the Dublin Society of the Arts organized the first design competition for children in 1745, manufacturers have strived to capture the appealing quality of improvisation in infant art. At the Atelier Martine in Paris, little girls designed "charming things" for the stylist Poiret who praised the "savage and natural manner" of one of his protégées, the author of a wheat-field motif. More recently, Sir Terence Conran's son Ned produced a design at the age of ten, which for several years was one of the Conran chain's top sellers. And now in the United States, the small Harlem Textile works, specializing in stylish upholstery fabrics for the home, has acquired patterns from local schoolchildren who "paint from the soul."

One of a series of fabrics by French designers Francis Miller and Patrick Bertaux, printed in bold blacks and grays on ecru cotton.

LEFT: *A wardrobe filled with antique Provençal fabrics, coverlets, petticoats, and cushions. Even the doors are lined in a faded striped cotton.* ABOVE: *A detail of an embroidered floral motif on a satin cotton.*

It seems appropriate that the vogue for figured fabrics initially took root in the French Midi, not far from the Mediterranean port of Marseilles—where, in the seventeenth century, traders first unbaled Indian chintzes. Although silk and cotton prints were eventually produced throughout Europe, in Provence they achieved early distinctive formal and chromatic qualities that have changed very little over the years. The brilliant hues and floral patterns of both Eastern textiles and their continental imitations reflected lush, sun-bathed landscapes and were illuminated by color combinations that ran the gamut from subtle to startling: emerald green flecked with vermilion, sea blue streaked with gold, muted fawn highlighted with cream. While eighteenth-century patrons generally abhorred somber, dark shades, their Victorian descendants appreciated deeply saturated tints. A special favorite was the low-maintenance *ramoneur* (chim-

a Provençal Collection

ney sweep), an obscure tone ideal for camouflaging dirt and wear. Patterns, too, were adapted to the dictates of current taste. Exuberant Eastern foliage was pruned and ordered with military precision such that, from a distance, blossoms, buds, and leaves often gave the impression of a strict geometric pattern. Once local designers had discarded the exotic comma-like *boteh* flower for more recognizable blooms (the tulip, the peony, the rose, even the humble daisy), the repertory of images remained stable. Initially, these quintessential Provençal fabrics were produced in a loose network of cottage ateliers, each with its own design or dye specialty. However, from the dawn of the industrial era through World War II, larger factories, notably *Les Olivades*, preserved the cloth that had become a visual synonym for continental country living.

Dorothée d'Orgeval and her husband, Jean, are connoisseurs of Provençal stuffs. "I don't like the term collector," Dorothée says, explaining that she merely "accumulates," selecting pieces for their intrinsic "charm, usefulness, and poetry." Most of her finds (which can be as small as a handkerchief or as large as a bedspread) embellish the stone-built home at Roussillon in the Vaucluse that has been in her family for generations.

In the d'Orgeval household patinated antique cottons and silks are intended for use rather than mere display. Plain white, patterned, and candy-striped fabrics hang on the walls, at windows, and across doorways. Bright squares are flung over gueridons; antique yellow silk furniture adorns the master bedroom; closets, drawers, and steamer trunks swing open to reveal cloth-lined interiors. The overflow is stacked in rustic cupboards for easy reference. Almost every piece still serves its original purpose. "I disapprove of recycling," Dorothée insists, "I hate to go against the original nature of any fabric, for example, to cut a minuscule cushion-case from a curtain." The only mutation she accepts is the relining of a coverlet with scraps that have been salvaged from treasured garments or trousseau items: "I find it touching that such trouble should be taken to save cherished relics."

The d'Orgevals' pride is a group of exquisitely stitched *boutis* (the traditional quilted coverlets), the most ancient of which date to the seventeenth century and are of the rare, vermiculated variety. Authentic *boutis "vermicelle"* are instantly recognizable by their intricate, cobwebby patterns in relief, created by inserting fine cords between the sewn outlines which join the two layers of fabric. Later quilts were simply wadded with cotton wool, producing a softer, more rounded effect, as well as greater warmth. Whether the material be patterned or plain, geometrical repeats of lozenges, parallel lines, wavelets, or interlocking circles are the most popular decorative motifs. Dorothée d'Orgeval prefers elaborately needleworked single-tone *boutis* in dusty pink, pale green, or white silk. She always looks for the symbols of marriage, good fortune, or happiness discreetly stitched into a corner: paired hearts and turtledoves, bouquets and garlands, entwined lovers' initials, or a once-memorable date. "These naive images of family bliss do not strike everyone between the eyes," she says. "But they do appeal irresistibly to the genuine *amateur*."

PRECEDING PAGES: *A beautiful red-and-white* boutis *rolled up on a cast-iron bed. The bedcover in indigo and white has an ikat effect. The pillows are covered in traditional mattress-ticking stripes.*

LEFT, CLOCKWISE FROM ABOVE FAR LEFT: *Exquisite fine quilting on a cotton coverlet. Tender fresh almonds in a ceramic lattice dish lie on another quilted* boutis. *Two reversible* boutis, *one silk, the other cotton. A reversible* boutis.

FOLLOWING PAGES, LEFT: *Simple mattress-ticking stripes reverse to plain red.* FOLLOWING PAGES, RIGHT: *A garden chair is shrouded in a reversible cotton* boutis.

glossary

baldaquin. A canopy or TESTER, suspended over a bed.

batik. "Wax writing" in Indonesian; a textile-printing method in which wax is used to protect patterned areas not to be dyed.

batiste. A fine, lightweight fabric, sometimes called CAMBRIC, usually of cotton.

batten. A flat, swordlike piece of wood with a sharp edge, used to beat down the WEFT on certain looms.

binding system. Weaving structure.

bistanclaque. A French term for a traditional manually operated loom.

block. A carved wood panel which, coated with dye, is pressed against a fabric to create a pattern.

bourette. A slightly coarse silk fabric with no luster.

broadcloth. A double-width woolen plain WEAVE, originally from the West Country in England.

brocade. An elaborately patterned compound WEAVE with additional WEFTS creating raised designs; originally woven from silk, today made from all fibers.

brocatelle. A WEAVE with two WARPS, resulting in slightly raised designs, mostly in SATIN against a plain ground.

buckram. A heavy linen or cotton cloth; used for backing softer, lighter fabrics or as window shades.

bullion. Thick twisted fringe, sometimes made from gold, silver, or metallic threads.

butterfly. A small fringe ornament.

calamanco. A sturdy cotton fabric resembling CHINTZ.

calico. A plain white or printed cotton cloth first imported from the Indian city of Calicut; the name has come to describe any cheap, printed cotton.

cambleteen. Low-quality CAMLET.

cambric. A fine, plain-weave cotton or linen fabric with a slight shine on the face side.

camlet. A plain-ribbed WEAVE that often combines different yarns with WORSTED.

cantonnière. Once a narrow hanging that covered bedposts; today refers to any drapery used to frame or decorate a window or door.

casein. A milk protein used in artificial fibers.

causeuse. A French sofa or chair for two, similar to the loveseat.

challis. A woolen fabric printed with a small floral design.

cheney. A brightly hued CAMLET, which is sometimes watered.

chenille. "Caterpillar" in French; sometimes referred to as "twice-woven" fabric; a fabric woven from woven yarn; its fuzzy pile makes it popular for use in coverlets.

chintz. From the Hindi *chitta;* originally a painted or printed Indian cloth; today, glazed cottons, often with floral designs.

cloqué. "Blistered" in French; refers to any fabric with a raised or puckered surface, such as SEERSUCKER.

corduroy. A heavy cotton or synthetic PILE fabric with regular ridges (wales).

LEFT: *Very rare and finely stitched coverlets, probably worked for a wedding trousseau.*

coutil. A strong, tightly woven cotton fabric made in a herringbone WEAVE and sometimes patterned.

cretonne. A ribbed, plain-weave fabric, made of linen or cotton.

dacron. A trade name for a resilient synthetic fiber commonly used for fillings and pillow stuffings.

damask. Originally a lustrous silk woven in Damascus; a reversible fabric of one or two colors in which figures are defined by the contrast of WEFT and WARP faced satin.

diaper. A compound WEAVE similar to LAMPAS in which the glossy WEFT forms a pattern against the plain ground.

dimity. From the Greek word for "double thread"; a fine cotton fabric made from double or triple yarns which create ridges.

dobby. A loom attachment that produces small geometric designs.

dralon. A trade name for an acrylic fiber commonly used for upholstery and in PILE fabrics; it is resistant to sunlight, unlike NYLON, and may be blended with other fabrics.

fagoted. A decorative trim created by pulling out horizontal threads from a fabric and gathering the remaining cross threads into an hourglass shape.

faille. A shimmery, closely woven cotton, rayon, or silk fabric distinguished by slightly raised ribs in the WEFT.

festoon. A decoration used in swagging fabrics.

fibranne. A French term for a VISCOSE staple fiber.

flax. The oldest known vegetable fiber comes from this plant; still commonly cultivated to make linen and linseed oil.

flounce. A scalloped fabric decorative edge.

fringe. Loose-hanging trim, often made of wool yarn, silk, or cotton twine.

furbelow. A gathered or ruffled piece of fabric.

fustian. A coarse cotton and linen TWILL with a nap.

gauffrage. See GOFFERING.

gimp. Braided trim.

gingham. A plain-weave cotton or POLYESTER fabric, usually yarn-dyed to create checks, stripes, or plaids.

ginning. The process of separating fibers from the seeds of the cotton plant in a cotton gin.

goffering. Indented or embossed surface finish achieved by compressing fabric between heated rollers; also known as GAUFFRAGE.

hackle. A heavy comb with long metal teeth, used in the dressing of FLAX, hemp, or JUTE.

heddle. A set of parallel strings or cords that separate WARP threads on a loom.

ikat. Fabric woven with resist-dyed WARP or WEFT.

"indiennes." Decorative cotton prints from India, first popular in France in the seventeenth century.

indigo. A deep-blue dye, originally obtained from plants of the *Indigofera* genus, cultivated in India; since the nineteenth century, replaced by synthetically produced aniline dye.

indiscret. A luxuriously upholstered circular settee with three places set back-to-back.

jacquard. Intricately patterned fabrics made from a mechanical loom; invented in France in 1800 by Joseph Marie Jacquard, the loom replaced "weaver's helpers" with a punch-card device, making it a one-man operation.

jasmin. A trim composed of several small linked elements.

jute. A bast fiber most often used for burlap, sacking, or twine.

lambrequin. PELMET over a window or door.

lamé. Any fabric containing metal yarns, usually gold or silver.

lampas. A compound WEAVE, usually in silk, in which supplementary WEFTS and WARPS are used to add colors to the face of the fabric, then tucked into the back.

madras. A plain-weave cotton fabric originally made in the Indian city of Madras; today, often brightly colored in check or square designs.

moiré. A ribbed fabric (usually silk or acetate) with a wavy, watered appearance produced by calendering. Moiré patterns can also be woven into the fabric.

moquette. A sturdy woolen WARP PILE fabric.

mordant. A chemical agent, usually a metallic salt, that fixes a dye to a fiber.

moreen. A variety of watered CAMLET.

muslin. A plain-weave cotton fabric varying in texture from fine and sheer to coarse.

nylon. A strong manmade fiber discovered in the United States in 1938; elastic and light-weight, it is derived from a POLYAMIDE resin.

orlon. A warm, absorbent, acrylic fiber often used with wool and other fibers.

ottoman. The late-eighteenth-century name for a low, upholstered, overstuffed sofa or footstool; also a heavy, stiff ribbed fabric with silk WARP, cotton WEFT.

panné velvet. Velvet or velour in which the PILE lies flat, creating a lustrous, polished surface.

pelmet. A piece of cloth or panel placed above a window or door to hide the top of a curtain or blind.

percale. A closely woven cotton fabric, similar to MUSLIN but finer; also referred to as BROADCLOTH.

pile. The downy face of a fabric such as velvet or velour, produced by an extra set of WEFT or WARP, forming raised loops which are cut.

pintadoe. From the Portuguese term for "spotted"; refers to painted or printed Indian cottons (see CHINTZ).

piqué. A strong silk, cotton, or RAYON fabric with a raised surface pattern.

plush. A soft, heavy fabric with even PILE closely resembling velvet; also referred to as velour and may be made from cotton, RAYON, wool, or silk.

point rentré. A weaver's method of obtaining chiaroscuro by interlocking threads of contrasting color to create an impression of relief.

polyamide. The resilient manmade fiber commonly referred to as NYLON.

polyester. Chemically produced fibers that are strong and wrinkle-resistant, but difficult to dye.

pongee. A thin, light fabric originally from China and woven in raw silk; today, plain or printed imitations are made from cotton or RAYON.

poplin. Originally a mixture of silk and wool, first woven in Avignon, the city of the popes; today a cotton fabric with horizontal ribs.

quilting. At least two layers of any fabric, joined with ornamental stitching and often padded with wool or down.

raffia. A strong bast fiber from the raffia palm, native to Madagascar.

rayon. A manmade fiber from wood or cotton cellulose.

resist-dyeing. A tinting process in which wax, clay, or simple knots are used to protect areas of the material so that it "resists" the dye, as in BATIK and tie-dyeing.

ret. To soak FLAX in order to loosen the fiber from the woody tissue.

rosette. A decorative fabric motif resembling a rose.

ruche. A gathered strip of fabric used in trimming.

satin. A plain WEAVE of Chinese origin with a smooth, lustrous face and a dull back.

satinette. A variation of satin WEAVE with a cotton WARP and wool WEFT; also an imitation or thin silk satin.

seersucker. A light Indian fabric originally of striped cotton or linen, with a "blistered" face achieved by altering tight and loose WARPS; today, a chemical treatment gives this puckered effect.

serge. A durable smooth-faced fabric made from WORSTED or woolen yarn, with a distinct diagonal rib on both faces.

shantung. A coarse silk fabric, originally from China.

spindle. Once a simple stick, now a long, slender pin onto which thread is twisted.

tabby. Plain weave, in which WARP and WEFT cross each other at right angles, used for a wide range of fabrics, such as TAFFETA, MUSLIN, and canvas.

taffeta. A crisp, plain-weave ribbed fabric.

tassel. A dangling decorative trim made of bunched yarn or cord.

tergal. A French-manufactured POLYAMIDE.

tester. A wooden frame for holding a canopy over the top of a bed, or the canopy itself.

ticking. A sturdy striped linen or cotton twill used for mattresses and pillows.

toile de jouy. A printed cotton fabric originally manufactured in the French town of Jouy-en-Josas, where Oberkampf set up his factory in 1760; known for lighthearted motifs depicting pleasures of the era as well as events of the day.

trellis. A coarsely woven fabric of triple thread or an arrangement of latticework.

trevira. A German-manufactured POLYAMIDE fiber.

tweed. A plain or TWILL WEAVE woolen fabric from Scotland.

twill. A basic WEAVE with a diagonal grain, obtained by floating the WEFT over and under several WARPS.

viscose. A soft, absorbent cellulose fiber made from wood pulp.

warp. A set of fixed threads set lengthwise on a loom.

warp print. A design printed on the WARP before WEAVING, resulting in a hazy image.

weaving. Interlacing WEFT and WARP to produce a fabric.

weft. The threads drawn through the WARP on a shuttle to produce a woven fabric; also referred to as filling and woof.

worsted. A smooth fabric made from carded and combed wool yarn.

source guide

HISTORIC HOUSES, CASTLES, and MUSEUMS

Belgium

National Flax Museum
4 Rue Etienne Sabbe
Courtrai
Tel. (56) 21 01 38
The story of linen in Flanders —from flax to textile.

France

Chateau de Bagatelle
131 Route de Paris
80100 Abbeville
A charmingly furnished, privately owned chateau.

Chateau de Roquetaillade,
    Monument Historique
Vicomte et Vicomtesse J.P.
    de Baritault du Carpia
Mazères
33210 Langon
Tel. (56) 63 24 16
A medieval fortress that was restored and decorated by Viollet-le-Duc in the nineteenth century.

Château et Musée National
    de Fontainebleau
77300 Fontainebleau
Tel. (64) 22 27 40
A royal and imperial residence, containing fine examples of period textiles and furniture.

Eco Musée de la Grande
    Lande
40630 Sabres
Tel. (58) 07 52 70
A nineteenth-century rural village, furnished with simple cotton textiles of the period.

Eco Musée, Maison de
    La Soie
Place du 8 Mai
30170 St Hyppolyte
    du Fort
Tel. (66) 77 66 42
A museum dedicated to the story of silk, from cocoon to textile.

Musée Charles Demery
39 Rue Proudhon
13150 Tarascon
Tel. (90) 91 08 80
The history of the Demery family as depicted through two centuries of Provençal prints.

Musée Condé, Château
    de Chantilly
Property of l'Institut
    de France
60500 Chantilly
Tel. (44) 57 08 00
The furnished residence of the princess of Condé.

Musée d'Art et d'Industrie
2 Place Louis Comte
42000 St. Etienne
Tel. (77) 33 04 85
A fine collection of fabric samples, passementerie, tools of the trade, and an unusual selection of historic looms.

Musée de la Passementerie
    Jonzieux
42660 St. Genest-Malifaux
Tel. (77) 39 91 92 or
    39 91 10
A fine collection of ribbons and passementerie.

Musée de la Toile de Jouy
Château de l'Eglantine
54 Rue Charles de Gaulle
78350 Jouy-en-Josas
Tel. (1) 39 56 48 64
The story of Christophe-Philippe Oberkampf and his famous printed cotton, toile de Jouy.

Musée de l'Homme
17 Place du Trocadero
75016 Paris
Tel. (1) 45 53 70 60
A collection of ethnic textiles.

Musée de l'Impression
    sur Etoffes
3 Rue des Bons Gens
68100 Mulhouse
Tel. (89) 45 51 20
A collection that includes more than four million printed textile samples from Alsace as well as an exceptional collection of printed scarfs, handkerchiefs, and indiennes.

Musée de Sens, Ancien
    Palais des Archevêques
Rue de la Resistance
89100 Sens
Tel. (86) 64 15 27
A museum housing the treasures of the cathedral of St Etienne: Byzantine, Persian, and coptic textiles from the fifth to the fourteenth century.

Musée des Arts Africains
    et Océaniens
293 Avenue Daumesnil
75012 Paris
Tel. (1) 43 43 14 54
A collection of exclusively ethnic textiles.

Musée des Arts Decoratifs
Palais du Louvre
107 Rue de Rivoli
75001 Paris
Tel. (1) 42 60 32 14
An array of textile designs and historic furnished rooms.

Musée des Arts de la Mode
    et du Textile
Palais du Louvre
109 Rue de Rivoli
75001 Paris
Tel. (1) 42 60 32 14
A fine collection of silks, printed cottons, embroidery, and passementerie.

Musée des Beaux Arts
    de Tours
Place Francois Sicard
37000 Tours
Tel. (47) 05 68 73
Eighteenth- and nineteenth-century silks and designs.

Musée Historique des
    Tissus
34 Rue de la Charité
69002 Lyon
Tel. (78) 37 15 05
A collection of historical textiles, mainly woven silks from Lyons.

Musée National de Château
    de Versailles et des
    Trianons
78000 Versailles
Tel. (1) 30 84 74 00
The Sun King's residence in all its splendor.

Musée National de la
    Voiture et du Tourisme
Château de Compiègne
60200 Compiègne
Tel. (44) 40 02 02
A historic collection of carriages and other means of transport, including Napoleon III's deep-buttoned train carriage.

Musée National du Château
    de Compiègne
60200 Compiègne
Tel. (44) 40 02 02
Re-creations of royal and late-imperial residence rooms and an exceptional collection of silks and upholstery.

Musées Nationaux des
    Châtaux de Malmaison
    et de Bois-Préau
Avenue du Château
92500 Rueil Malmaison
Tel. (1) 47 49 20 07
The furnished residence of Napoleon I and Empress Joséphine.

Musée Pincé
32 bis Rue Lenepveau
49100 Angers
Tel. (41) 88 94 27
*A small collection
of eighteenth-century
Chinese silks.*

Great Britain

Bradford Industrial Museum
Moorside Road
Eccleshill, West Yorkshire
Tel. (0274) 631 756
*A mill, with textiles relative
to the local woolen industry.*

The Burrell Collection
Pollock Country Park
Glasgow G43 1AT
Scotland
Tel. (041) 649 7151
*A rich collection of decorative
arts, including textiles,
donated to Glasgow by Sir
William and Lady Burrell.*

Burton Constable Hall
Nr Hull
North Humberside
North Yorkshire
HU11 4LN
Tel. (0964) 562 400
*A magnificent Elizabethan
house containing exceptional
furnishings.*

Buscot Park
Nr Faringdon,
Oxfordshire SN7 8BU
*Contents and furnishings of
this eighteenth-century house.*

Castle Coole
Property of The National
    Trust
Enniskillen
County Fermanagh,
Northern Ireland
Tel. (0365) 322 690
*A magnificent eighteenth-
century mansion, lavishly
refurbished (with some of the
original textiles and trim)
by the National Trust.*

Charleston Farmhouse
The Charleston Trust
Nr Firele Lewes
East Sussex BN86LL
Tel. (0323) 811 265

*The house and contents
decorated by Omega artists
Vanessa Bell and Duncan
Grant, who lived there
from 1916 until Grant's
death in 1978.*

Chatsworth
Chatsworth House Trust
    Bakewell
Derbyshire DE4 1PP
Tel. (0246) 582 204
*The palatial residence of the
Duke and Duchess of
Devonshire. The splendors
include five virtually unaltered
seventeenth-century state rooms.*

Ham House
National Trust/Victoria &
    Albert Museum
Richmond
Surrey TW10 7RS
Tel. (081) 940 1950
*Built in the 1670s, this
remarkable house still contains
most of its period furnishings
from that period, and many
of the original silks.*

Highclere Castle
Nr Newbury
Berkshire RG15 9RN
Tel. (0635) 253 210
*The Victorian country home of
Lord and Lady Carnarvon,
recently restored and redecorated
by the owners.*

Knole
Property of The National
    Trust
Sevenoaks
Kent TN15 ORP
Tel. (0732) 450 608
*The home of the Sackville-
Wests, dating mainly from
the fifteenth century, and
containing a fine collection of
seventeenth-century furniture
and early textiles.*

Leeds Castle
Leeds Castle Foundation
Nr Maidstone
Kent ME17 1PL
Tel. (0622) 765 400
*A fairytale castle of the
medieval queens of England.
Contains exceptional
furnishings.*

Museum of Leeds;
    Armley Mills
Canal Road
Armley, West Yorkshire
Tel. (0532) 637 861
*A vast 1806 woolen mill,
housing period textiles, a
water wheel, and printing
machinery.*

Museum of Mankind
6 Burlington Gardens
London W1X 2EX
Tel. (071) 437 2224
*A great resource for ethnic
textiles.*

Paradise Silk Museum
Old Park Lane
Macclesfield, Cheshire
Tel. (0625) 618 228
*A museum specializing
in the history, textiles,
and industry tools of silk
weaving on hand looms.*

Quarry Bank Mill
The National Trust/Quarry
    Bank Mill Trust Ltd.
Styal, Cheshire
Tel. (0625) 527 468
*This eighteenth-century
working mill shows all aspects
of the cotton industry from
water wheel to woven cloth.*

Scottish Museum of
    Woollen Textiles
Tweedvale Mill
Walkerburn
Scotland EH43 6AH
Tel. (089 687) 281
The story of the wool industry.

Scottish Tartans Museum
Comrie
Tayside
Scotland PH6 2DW
Tel. (0764) 70779
*Special treats, including
a myriad of tartans and a
weaver's cottage.*

Victoria & Albert Museum
South Kensington
London SW7 2RL
Tel. (071) 938 8500
*A magnificent collection of
decorative arts from early
Christian times to the present,
including exceptional textiles.*

William Morris Gallery
Water House
Lloyd Park, Forest Road
Walthamstow E17 4PP
Tel. (071) 527 5544
*Furniture, textiles, and
personal mementoes of Morris
and his entourage, housed in
his childhood home.*

India

The Calico Museum
Ahmadabad, Gujerat
*A prestigious display of
fabrics, including painted
toiles, rare cottons, and
moghul silks—appropriate to
a city whose past wealth was
founded on three fibers: gold,
silk, and cotton.*

Italy

Ca' Rezzonico
Museo del Settecento
    Veneziano
Grand Canal, Venice
*Venice's collection of
eighteenth-century art
displayed in magnificently
furnished rooms.*

Museo Fortuny
Palazzo Fortuny
San Marco, 3780
Campo San Beneto
30124 Venice
*Fortuny's textiles displayed
in his studio.*

Palazzo Pitti
Florence
Tel. (055) 21 34 40
*Italy's premiere collection of
historic costumes and textiles.*

Museo Nazionale
Palazzo Mansi
Via Galli Tassi 43
55100 Lucca
Tel. (0583) 55 570
*Over five hundred samples of
sixteenth- and seventeenth-
century silks and velvets
woven in Lucca.*

L'Instituto Tecnico
    Industriale "T. Buzzi"
Viale della Republica 9
50047 Prato, Florence
Tel. (0574) 57 03 52
*A permanent exhibition of
textiles for clothing ranging
from the fifteenth to the
nineteenth century. (Until
very recently, textiles used
for clothing were the same
as those used for furnishings.)*

Casa Da Noal
Via Canova 7
Treviso
Tel. (0422) 51 337
*Italian textiles and costumes
from the fourteenth through
the nineteenth century.*

Museo Egizio
Via Accademia Delle
    Scienze 6
Turin
Tel. (011) 56 17 776
*Textiles of pharaohnic Egypt,
including pleated tunics, as
well as coptic weaves.*

Sweden

Gripsholm Castle
Property of the Royal
    Collection, Stockholm
Mariefred
Tel. (0159) 10 194
*A sixteenth-century palace,
equipped with full period
furnishings.*

Skogaholm Manor,
    Skansen Museum
11593 Stockholm
Tel. (8) 67 00 20
*A seventeenth-century manor,
refurbished in the late
Gustavian style in 1793.*

Textile Museum
Druvefortsvägen 8
50256 Borås
Tel. (033) 168950
*A detailed look at the
cultural, technical, and
industrial history of textiles.*

Von Echstedt Manor
Property of the Värmlands
    Museum
Box 335
Karlstad
*An eighteenth-century Rococo
manor, in country style.*

Switzerland

Fondation Abegg
CH 3132 Riggisberg
Bern
Tel. (31) 80 12 01
*An exceptional textile archive.
By appointment only.*

United States

Art Institute of Chicago
Michigan Avenue &
    Adams Street
Chicago, IL 60603
Tel. (312) 443-3600
*The Art Institute's Western
Textile Collection includes
tapestries, coverlets, and
woven materials from France,
Italy, and Peru. The museum
also has an excellent library
for research on textiles.*

Brooklyn Museum of Art
200 Eastern Parkway
Brooklyn, NY 11238
Tel. (718) 638-5000
*This institution's huge
Costume and Textile
department has a collection
of over 25,000 textiles
from around the world.*

Colonial Williamsburg
    Foundation
Goodwin Building
P.O. Box 1776
Williamsburg, VA 23185
Tel. (804) 229-1000
*Colonial Williamsburg is
dedicated to preserving
the history and heritage
of the Williamsburg
colony. The collection has
outstanding examples of
American material culture.*

Cooper-Hewitt National
    Museum of Design
Smithsonian Institution
2 East 91st Street
New York, NY 10029
Tel. (212) 860-6868

*An extensive and varied
collection of textiles, design
drawings, and artifacts
from all eras.*

Fashion Institute of
    Technology
Seventh Avenue at 27th
    Street
New York, NY 10001
Tel. (212) 760-7970
*A wide collection of
swatches, jacquard samples,
and both period and
contemporary textiles.*

Helen Louise Allen
    Textile Collection
1300 Linden Drive
University of Wisconsin
Madison, WI 53706
Tel. (608) 262-1162
*Twelve hundred-plus
textile samples, including
archeological textiles, fifteenth-
to eighteenth-century historic
textiles, eighteenth- and
nineteenth-century American
and European coverlets,
eighteenth- to twentieth-century
furnishings and fabric.*

Henry Francis du Pont
    Winterthur Museum, Inc.
Route 52
Winterthur, DE 19735
Tel. (305) 888-4600
*Winterthur houses one of the
largest and finest collections
of American decorative arts
in the world.*

Historic Deerfield, Inc.
The Street
Deerfield, MA 01342
Tel. (413) 774-5581
*This village of eighteenth-
and nineteenth-century
historic-house museums has
excellent examples of American
material culture.*

Indianapolis Museum of Art
1200 West 38th Street
Indianapolis, IN 46208
Tel. (317) 923-1331
*A collection of over 7,000
examples of various weaves;
particularly strong in Oriental
and European textiles.*

Mount Vernon—Ladies
    Association of the Union
End of George Washington
    Parkway South
Mount Vernon, VA 22121
Tel. (703) 780-2000
*A fine collection of textiles, both
period pieces and reproductions.*

Museum of American
    Textile History
800 Massachusetts Avenue
North Andover, MA 01845
Tel. (508) 686-0191
*Industry periodicals, sample
books, and tools of the trade.*

Museum of Fine Arts
465 Huntington Avenue
Boston, MA 02115
Tel. (617) 267-9300
*One of the largest textile
museums in the United States.*

Old Sturbridge Village
1 Old Sturbridge Village
    Road
Sturbridge, MA 01566
Tel. (508) 347-3362
*A historic village depicting
life in eighteenth-century
New England.*

Paley Design Center of the
    Philadelphia College of
    Textiles and Science
4200 Henry Avenue
Philadelphia, PA 19144
Tel. (215) 951-2860
Textiles and related tools.

Peabody Museum of
    Archaeology and
    Ethnology
11 Divinity Avenue
Cambridge, MA 02138
Tel. (617) 495-2248
*A collection focusing on objects
from the preindustrial cultures
of North America, South
America, and Asia.*

Scalamandre Center for
    Decorative Arts Research
37-24 24th Street
Long Island City, N.Y. 11101
Tel. (718) 361-8500
*The history of Scalamandre
family and firm, including
examples of ca. 1500s
textiles, ca. 1750s wall
coverings, and passementerie.*

Senate House State
   Historic Site
312 Fair Street
Kingston, NY 12401
Tel. (914) 338-2786
*Fine eighteenth- to nineteenth-
century furnishings on display.*

The Shaker Museum
   and Library
Shaker Museum Road
Old Chatham, NY 12136
Tel. (518) 794-9100
Shaker textiles and tools.

Textile Study Room, The
   Metropolitan Museum
Fifth Avenue at 82nd Street
New York, NY 10028
Tel. (212) 879-5500
*A wide collection of textiles,
sample books, and tools.*

Textile Museum
2320 S St. N.W.
Washington, D.C. 20008
Tel. (202) 607-0441
*Over 1,400 examples of
international textiles.*

Thousand Islands Craft
   School Textile Museum
314 John Street
Clayton, NY 13624
Tel. (315) 686-4123
Library, textiles, and tools.

Victoria Mansion
109 Danforth Street
Portland, ME 04101
Tel. (207) 772-4841
*Furnishings commissioned by
Gustave Herter.*

TEXTILE
MANUFACTURERS

France

Shyam Ahuja
5 Passage de la Petite
   Boucherie
75006 Paris
Tel. (1) 43 26 20 46
Indian cottons and silks.

Bianchini Férier
4 Rue Vaucanson
69001 Lyon
Tel. (78) 28 02 43

*Specializes in printed silks,
houses a magnificent archive.*

Le Crin
45 Rue de Sèvres
75006 Paris
Tel. (1) 45 44 71 40
*Offers lovely horsehair textiles
woven on traditional looms.*

Prelle
5 Place des Victoires
75001 Paris
Tel. (1) 42 36 67 21
*Specializes in silk damasks
and lampas; houses an
extensive private archive.*

Tassinari & Chatel
26 Rue Danielle Casanova
75002 Paris
Tel. (1) 42 61 74 08
*Creates stunning silks and
receives special commissions.*

Great Britain

John Boyd Textiles
Higher Flax Mills
Castle Cary, Somerset
Tel. (0963) 50 451
*Another horsehair
textiles source.*

Gainsborough Silk Weaving
   Co., Ltd.
Alexandra Road
Chilton
Sudbury
Suffolk CO10 6XH
Tel. (0787) 72 081
*An excellent source for
traditional silk weaves.*

Park Mill
Holcombe Road
Helmshore
Rossendale, Lancashire
Tel. (0706) 229 341
*Reproductions of antique
fabrics and trim.*

Warner Fabrics
7–11 Noel Street
London W1
Tel. (071) 439 2411
*Specializes in cottons and
silks, and houses a font of
information in its archives.*

Italy

Luigi Bevilacqua
S. Croce 1320
30135 Venice
Tel. (041) 72 13 84
*Weaves silks, damasks, and
velvets on traditional looms.*

Ratti
Villa Sucota
22100 Como
Tel. (031) 23 31 11
Creates superb silk weaves.

Lorenzo Rubelli
Palazzo Corner Spinelli
3877 San Marco
30124 Venice
and
c/o Bergamo
D&D Building
979 Third Avenue
17th floor
New York, NY 10022
Tel. (212) 883-3333
*Produces magnificent silks and
velvets on traditional looms.*

United States

Brunschwig & Fils
979 Third Avenue
New York, NY 10022
Tel. (212) 838-7878

Cowtan & Tout, Inc.
979 Third Avenue
New York, NY 10022
Tel. (212) 753-4488

Decorator's Walk
160 East 56th Street
New York, NY 10022
Tel. (212) 355-5300

F. Schumacher & Company
79 Madison Avenue
New York, NY 10016
Tel. (212) 213-7900

Scalamandre Silk, Inc.
950 Third Avenue
New York, NY 10022
Tel. (212) 980-3888

Rose Cumming, Inc.
232 East 59th Street
New York, NY 10022
Tel. (212) 758-0844

Lee Jofa, Inc.
979 Third Avenue
New York, NY 10022
Tel. (212) 688-0444

Clarence House Fabrics, Ltd.
211 East 59th Street
New York, NY 10022
Tel. (212) 752-2890

DECORATORS

France

Christian Benais
9 Rue de Clichy
75009 Paris
Tel. (1) 48 78 21 19

Agnes Comar
7 Avenue George V
75008 Paris
Tel. (1) 47 23 33 85

Jacques Garcia
212 Rue de Rivoli
75001 Paris
Tel. (1) 42 97 48 70

Elisabeth Garouste et
   Mattia Bonetti
c/o En Attendant Les
   Barbares
50 Rue Etienne Marcel
75002 Paris
Tel. (1) 42 33 37 87

François Josef Graf
17 Rue de Lille
75007 Paris
Tel. (1) 42 61 39 39

Jacques Grange
118 FBG St. Honoré
75008 Paris
Tel. (1) 47 42 47 34

Miller et Bertaux
27 Rue du Bourg Tibourg
75004 Paris
Tel. (1) 42 77 25 31

Jean-Louis Riccardi
32 Rue Vineuse
75016 Paris
Tel. (1) 47 27 07 76

Great Britain

Nina Campbell
9 Walton Street
London SW3 2JD
Tel. (071) 225-1011

Colefax & Fowler
39 Brook Street
London W1
Tel. (071) 493-2231

United States

Mario Buatta
120 East 80th Street
New York, NY 10021
Tel. (212) 988-6811

Robert Couturier
138 West 25th Street
New York, NY 10001
Tel. (212) 463-7177

David Easton
323 East 58th Street
New York, NY 10022
Tel. (212) 486-6704

Mark Hampton
654 Madison Avenue
New York, NY 10021
Tel. (212) 753-4110

William Hodgins
232 Clarendon Street
Boston, MA 02116
Tel. (617) 262-9538

Parish-Hadley Associates
305 East 63rd Street
New York, NY 10021
Tel. (212) 888-7979

John Saladino
305 East 63rd Street
New York, NY 10021
Tel. (212) 752-2440

Bunny Williams
4 East 77th Street
New York, NY 10021
Tel. (212) 772-8585

Vincent Wolf
400 East 52nd Street
New York, NY 10022
(212) 355-6581

DESIGNERS

Belgium

Anne Beetz
28 Rue de L'Arbre Bénit
1050 Brussels
Tel. (2) 511 2138

France

Christian Astuguevieille
"Ficelleries"
42 Galerie Vivienne
75002 Paris
Tel. (1) 42 94 00 08

Robert Le Héros
15 Rue Tiquetonne
75002 Paris
Tel. (1) 40 41 92 93

Great Britain

Nigel Atkinson Textiles
4 Camden Square
London NW1
Tel. (071) 284 0316

Bentley & Spens
Studio 25
90 Lots Road
London W10 OQD
Tel. (071) 352 5685

Ruth Harjula & Colin
    Chetwood
The Coach House
West Mill Lane
Hitchin, Hertsforshire
Tel. (0462) 422 118

Carolyn Quartermaine
London
Tel. (071) 373 4492

Timney Fowler
388 Kings Road
London SW3 5UZ
Tel. (071) 352 2263

Italy

Norélène
2606 San Marco
Campo San Maurizio
Venice
Tel. (041) 523 7605

United States

Manuel Canovas
136 East 57th Street
New York, NY 10022
Tel. (212) 486-9230

Christopher Hyland
979 Third Avenue
New York, NY 10022
Tel. (212) 688-6121

Jack Lenor Larsen
41 East 11th Street
New York, NY 10033
(212) 674-3993

Motif Designs
20 Jones Street
New Rochelle, NY 10801
Tel. (914) 633-1170

PASSEMENTERIE

France

Houles
18 Rue Saint Nicolas
75012 Paris
Tel. (1) 43 44 65 19

La Passementerie Nouvelle
15 Rue Etienne Marcel
75002 Paris
Tel. (1) 42 36 30 01

Passementeries de l'Ile
    de France
11 Rue Trousseau
75001 Paris
Tel. (1) 48 05 44 33

Edmond Petit/Chandet
19 Rue du Mail
75002 Paris
Tel. (1) 45 08 06 44

Great Britain

Colefax & Fowler
39 Brook Street
London W1
Tel. (071) 493 2231

G.J. Turner (trade only)
Fitzroy House
Abbot Street
London E8
Tel. (071) 254 8187

Wemyss Houles
40 Newman Street
London W1
Tel. (071) 255 3305

United States

André Bon
979 Third Avenue
New York, NY 10022
Tel. (212) 355-4012

Clarence House
979 Third Avenue
New York, NY 10022
Tel. (212) 752-2890

Houlés, Inc.
854 Melrose Avenue
Los Angeles, CA 90069
Tel. (310) 652-6171

M & J Trimming
1008 Sixth Avenue
New York, NY 10018
Tel. (212) 391-9072

Old World Weavers
979 Third Avenue
New York, NY 10022
Tel. (212) 355-7186

Passementerie
979 Third Avenue
New York, NY 10022
Tel. (212) 355-7600

Scalamandre
950 Third Avenue
New York, NY 10022
Tel. (212) 980-3888

Standard Trimming Co.
306 East 62nd Street
New York, NY 10021
Tel. (212) 355-4012

GILDED FINIALS,
CURTAIN
TIE-BACKS, ETC.

Clare Mosley
56 Camberwell Grove
London SE 5
Great Britain
Tel. (071) 708 3123

PRINTS

France

Fornasetti
L'Eclaireur
3 ter Rue des Rosiers
75004 Paris
Tel. (1) 48 87 10 22

Souleiado
Ets Charles Demery
39 Rue Proudhon
13140 Tarascon
Tel. (90) 91 08 80

Great Britain

William Morris
Liberty of London
210/220 Regent Street
London WI
Tel. (071) 734 1234

Italy

Fortuny
V. Trois
San Marco 2666
Campo San Maurizio
Venice
Tel. (041) 522 2905

United States

Laura Ashley, Inc.
714 Madison Avenue
New York, NY 10021
Tel. (212) 735-5010

Cowtan & Tout, Inc.
979 Third Avenue
New York, NY 10022
Tel. (212) 753-4488

Liberty of London, Inc.
108 West 39th Street
New York, NY 10018
Tel. (212) 391-2150

Pierre Deux Fabrics
870 Madison Avenue
New York, NY 10021
Tel. (212) 570-9343

J. Schumacher & Company
79 Madison Avenue
New York, NY 10016
Tel. (212) 213-7900

OLD TEXTILES

France

L'Appartement
21 Rue Jacob
75006 Paris
Tel. (1) 43 25 87 69

L'Autre Jour (Dorothée &
    Jean d'Orgeval)
26 Ave. de la Bourdonnais
75007 Paris
Tel. (1) 47 05 36 60

Aux Fils du Temps
33 Rue de Grenelle
75007 Paris
Tel. (1) 45 48 14 68

Michel Biehn
7 Avenue des Quatre Otages
84800 L'Isle-Sur-la-Sorgue
Tel. (90) 20 89 04

Fanette
1 Rue d'Alençon
75015 Paris
Tel. (1) 42 22 21 73

Galerie Epoca
    (Mony Linz Einstein)
60 Rue de Verneuil
75007 Paris
Tel. (1) 45 49 21 48

Guatemala Weaves
    (Marina Biras)
5 Rue Lobineau
75006 Paris
Tel. (1) 43 25 01 64

Les Indiennes
10 Rue St Paul
75004 Paris
Tel. (1) 42 72 35 34

Vivement Jeudi
52 Rue Mouffetard
75005 Paris
Tel. (1) 43 31 44 52

Great Britain

Joanna Booth
247 Kings Road
London SW3 5EL
Tel. (071) 352 8998

S. Franses
82 Jermyn Street
St James
London SW1
Tel. (071) 235 1888

Fulham 72
72 Fulham Road
London SW3
Tel. (071) 225 0385

Gallery of Antique Costume
    and Textiles
2 Church Street
London NW8
Tel. (071) 723 9981

Christophe Gollut
116 Fulham Road
London SW3
Tel. (071) 370 4101

Judy Greenwood Antiques
657 Fulham Road
London SW3
Tel. (071) 736 6037

Linda Gumb
9 Camden Passage
London N1
Tel. (071) 354 1184

Heraz
25 Motcomb Street
London SW1
Tel. (071) 235 7416

Paul Jones
569 Kings Road
London SW3
Tel. (071) 371 8062

Christopher Moore
38 Ledbury Road
London W11
Tel. (071) 792-3628

Sweden

Boutique Louisa Ulrika
Köpmangatan 9
Stockholm
Tel. (8) 203703

Lena Rahoult
Nybrogatan 25
114 39 Stockholm
Tel. (8) 6605030
By appointment only.

Gamla Saker
Hjälmaröd 3, Kivik
Tel. 414 705 15

United States

David Bernstein Fine Art
737 Park Avenue
New York, NY 10021
Tel. (212) 794-0389

Margaret E. Geiss-Mooney
1124 Cielia Court
Petaluma, CA 94954
Tel. (707) 763-8694
Textile conservator.

Cora Ginsburg
19 East 74th Street
New York, NY 10021
Tel. (212) 744-1352
By appointment.

Renate Halpern Galleries
325 East 79th Street
New York, NY 10022
Tel. (212) 988-9316
By appointment.

Lotus Collection
500 Pacific Avenue
San Francisco, CA 94113
Tel. (415) 398-8115

Ghiordan Knot Ltd.
136 East 57th Street
New York, NY 10022
Tel. (212) 371-6390

Schmul Meier
23 Main Street
Tarrytown, NY 10591
Tel. (914) 332-1310
Tel. (212) 644-8590
Contact: David Hammond

Textile Arts Gallery
1571 Canyon Road
Santa Fe, NM 87501
Tel. (505) 983-9780

Joseph Toorian
1240 East Colorado Blvd.
Pasadena, CA 91106
Tel. (818) 934-9308

bibliography

In addition to the many books available on textiles, many periodicals provide information on their history, design, and decorative uses. Of particular scholarly interest are *The Textile Museum Journal* (Washington, D.C.) and *Hali* (London/New York). *The World of Interiors, Vogue,* and *L'Atelier* provide up-to-date information on contemporary trends in decorating and design.

Ala Napoleonica e Museo Correr. *I mestieri della moda a Venezia dal XIII al XVIII secolo.* Venice, 1988.

Baines, P. *Linen: Hand Spinning and Weaving.* London, 1989.

Baker, G. P., & J. Ltd. *From East to West.* London, 1984.

Barnard, N. *Living with Decorative Textiles.* London, 1989.

Baudot, F. *Les Assises du siècle.* Paris, 1990.

Bell, Q., et al. *Charleston Past & Present.* London, 1987.

Bergamaschi, G. *Fior di Lino.* Milan, 1985.

Biehn, M. *En Jupon piqué et robe d'indienne.* Paris, 1987.

Bourget, P. *Tissus coptes.* Angers, n.d.

Bredif, J. *Toiles de Jouy.* Paris, 1989.

Brunhammer, Y. *1925.* Paris, 1976.

Buseghin, M. L., ed. *In viaggio con Penelope.* Milan, 1989.

Bussagli, M., et al. *Arte del Tessere.* Rome, 1987.

Calloway, S. *L'Epoque et son style: La Décoration interieure au XXe siècle.* Paris, 1988.

Canovas, M. *Le Guide des tissus d'ameublement.* Paris, 1986.

Centro Italiano per lo Studio della Storia del Tessuto, ed. *Aspetti e problemi degli studi sui tessili antichi.* Turin, 1983.

———— *I tessili antichi e il loro uso.* Turin, 1986.

Chevalier, J., and A. Gheerbrant. *Dictionnaire des symboles.* Paris, 1989.

Clabburn, P. *Furnishing Textiles.* London, 1989.

Clifton-Mogg, C., and M. Paine. *The Curtain Book.* London, 1989.

Coural, J. *Paris, Mobilier national: Soieries Empire.* Paris, 1980.

Davidson, C. *The World of Mary Ellen Best.* London, 1985.

Desai, C. *Ikat Textiles of India.* London, 1989.

Dewilde, B. *Flax in Flanders Throughout the Centuries.* Thielt, 1987.

Dupont-Auberville, M. *Classic Textile Designs.* London, 1989.

Edwards, R. *The Shorter Dictionary of English Furniture.* London, 1964.

Fowler, J., and J. Cornforth. *English Decoration in the 18th Century.* London, 1986.

Fraser, J. *The Golden Bough.* New York, 1951.

Garrett, E. D. *At Home: The American Family 1750–1870.* New York, 1990.

Gere, C. *L'Epoque et son style: La Décoration intérieure au XIXe siècle.* Paris, 1989.

Grow, L. *The Old House Book of Living Rooms and Parlors.* New York, 1980.

Harvey, P. *The Oxford Companion to Classical Literature.* Oxford, 1962.

Hecht, A. *The Art of the Loom.* London, 1989.

Huette, R. *Le Livre de la passementerie.* Dourdan, n.d.

Hugues, P. *Le Langage du tissu.* Le Havre, 1982.

Jelmini, J. P. et al., ed. *La Soie.* Neuchâtel, 1986.

Jones, C. *Colefax & Fowler.* London, 1989.

Kolander, C. *A Silk Worker's Notebook.* Loveland Co., 1985.

Kron, Joan. *Home-Psych: The Social Psychology of Home and Decoration.* New York, 1980.

Larsen, Jack Lenor. *Furnishing Fabrics: An International Handbook.* London, 1989.

Luc-Benoist. *Les Tissus, la tapisserie, les tapis.* Paris, 1926.

Martiniani-Reber, M. *Lyon, Musée historique des tissus: Soieries sassanides, coptes et byzantines V–XI siècles.* Paris, 1986.

Mayer Thurman, C. "Neoclassicism on Cloth." *The Art Institute of Chicago Museum Studies,* vol. 15, no 1. Chicago, 1989.

McWilliams, M. A. "Prisoner Imagery in Safavid Textiles." *The Textile Museum Journal 1987.* Washington, D.C., 1988.

Mendes, V. *Novelty Fabrics.* London, 1988.

Miller, J. and M. *Period Style.* London, 1989.

Murphy, V. *Indian Floral Patterns.* London, 1985.

Musée de l'Impression sur Etoffes de Mulhouse. *Toiles de Nantes des XVIIIe et XIXe siècles.* Mulhouse, 1978.

Musée Oberkampf. *Christophe-Philippe Oberkampf et la Manufacture de Jouy-en-Josas.* Colmar, 1987.

National Gallery of Art. *The Fashioning and Functioning of the British Country House.* Washington, D.C., 1989.

Origo, I. *The Merchant of Prato.* London, 1963.

Osma, F. de. *Mariano Fortuny: His Life and Work.* New York, 1980.

Parry, L. *Textiles of the Arts and Crafts Movement.* London, 1988.

———. *William Morris and the Arts & Crafts Movement.* London, 1989.

Pastoureau, M. *L'Etoffe du Diable.* Paris, 1991.

Pitoiset, G. *Toiles imprimées XVIIIe–XIXe siècles.* Paris, 1982.

Polo, Marco. *The Travels.* Trans. R. Latham. London, 1958.

Praz, M. *La filosofia dell'arredamento.* Milan, 1981.

Rense, P. *Decorating for Celebrities.* New York, 1980.

Riccioni, G. *Tessitori e Tappezzieri.* Florence, 1989.

Rothstein, N. *Spitalfields Silks.* London, 1975.

———. *Silk Designs of the Eighteenth Century.* London, 1990.

Roux, A. *Les Tissus d'art.* Paris, 1931.

Rybczynski, W. *Home: A Short History of an Idea.* New York, 1986.

Schoeser, M., and K. Dejardin. *Tissus français d'ameublement de 1760 à nos jours.* Paris, 1991.

Schoeser, M., and C. Rufey. *English and American Textiles from 1790 to the Present.* London, 1989.

Schrader, W. *Les Soieries anciennes d'Asie.* Paris, 1962.

Spink & Son Ltd. *The Art of Textiles.* London, 1989.

Sutton, A., and D. Sheehan. *Ideas in Weaving.* Loveland Co., 1988.

Thornton, P. *Authentic Decor: The Domestic Interior 1620–1920.* London, 1985.

Tomlin, M. *Ham House.* London, 1986.

Vallance, A. *The Life and Work of William Morris.* London, 1986.

Wadsworth Atheneum. *French Textiles from the Middle Ages Through the Second Empire.* Hartford, Conn., 1985.

Wainwright, C. *The Romantic Interior.* New Haven, 1989.

Warner & Sons Ltd. *A Choice of Design 1850–1980.* N.p., 1981.

Weigert, R. A. *Tessuti d'arte europei epoca Luigi XV.* Milan, 1965.

Weiner, A., and J. Schneider, eds. *Cloth and the Human Experience.* Washington, D.C., 1989.

Wilson, K. *A History of Textiles.* Boulder, Col., 1979.

Yang, S., and R. Narasin. *Textile Art of Japan.* Tokyo, 1989.

acknowledgments

As the authors of this book, we do not pretend to be experts in fabric and fabric design. We are simply amateurs, in both senses of the word: we have never studied textiles professionally, but through our work with magazines (Caroline as stylist and Jacques as photographer), we have come to love the beauty and versatility of fabrics.

It has been our good fortune to discover many of these locations while on assignment for various magazines. We owe our thanks to them, along with the many kind and generous people who opened up museums, archives, castles, homes, attics, and closets to offer us a glimpse of the fascinating world of fabrics.

With apologies to all those we may inadvertently omit, we express our particular gratitude, first and foremost to Nancy Novogrod, to whom we owe the original idea for this book; to our editor, Lauren Shakely, who suffered many months of transatlantic correspondence and always gave us her encouragement and her valuable advice; and to all those at Clarkson Potter who helped us on the way: Lindsey Crittenden, Joan Denman, Mark McCauslin, Jane Treuhaft, and Kristin Frederickson. And for her beautiful design for the book, we thank Dania Martinez Davey.

Also to Alidad, Michèle Aragon, Nick Ashley, Christian Astuguevieille, Pompon Bailhache, Christian Benais, Kim Bentley and Sally Spens, Luigi Bevilacqua, Bianchini-Férier, Catherine and Michel Biehn, Mattia Bonetti, Marie-France Boyer, Josette Bredif, Judy Brittain, Jacques Campistron, Ca' Rezzonico, David Champion, The Charleston Trust, Marianne Chedid, Agnès Comar, Jean-Pierre Demery, Dick Dumas, Marie-Claude Dumoulin, Paul Duncan, Michaela Dunworth, Ecomusée de la Grande Lande, Mony Linz Einstein, Eliakim, Lady Faringdon, Marion Faver, Hélène and Roberto Feruzzi, Bibliothèque Forney, Grahame Fowler, Jacques Garcia, Emile Garcin, César Garçon, Elisabeth Garouste, Mary Goodwin, Jacques Grange, Josephine Grever, Gripsholm Castle, Tricia Guild, Nelly Guyot, Christine and Denis Hadey, Ham House, The Hancock Museum, Ruth Harjula, Takahashi Hisachika, Julian Humphrey, Jacqueline Jacqué of the Musée de l'Impression sur Etoffes, Marie Kalt, Jean-François Keller, Françoise Labro, John Laflin, Karl Lagerfeld, Leeds Castle, Amélie Lefebure of the Musée Condé, Richard Stuart Liberty, Florence Lopez, La Maison du Lin, Renzo Mongiardino, Pascal Morabito, Amicia de Moubray, J. S. Mus, Musée de la Voiture et du Tourisme, Museo Fortuny, Isabella Napolitano, The National Flax Museum, Nobilis, Dorothée and Jean d'Orgeval, Marie-Claude Orsoni, La Passementerie Nouvelle, Roberto Pedrina, J. P. Piter, Prelle, Carolyn Quartermaine, Lena Rahoult, Jean-Louis Riccardi, Robert Le Héros, Rubelli, Mary Sargent-Ladd, Mary Schoeser, Skansen Museum, Yves Germain Taralon, Tassinari and Chatel, Françoise Teynac, Vincent Thfoin, Sue Timney, Vårmlands Museum, Madame de Wailly, The Warner Archive, and Deborah Webster.

photo credits

All photographs in this book are by Jacques Dirand except:
Bibliothèque Forney: 26.
Jean-Loup Charmet: 1, 2, 3, 6, 7, 12 excluding bottom right, 32, 39, 86.
Giraudon: 67, 87.
The Warner Archive: 184.

Photographs by Jacques Dirand by courtesy of the following:
Bianchini Férier: 10, 13, 14–15, 55, 70, 83, 182 (top left and bottom), 183.
Bibliothèque de l'Arsenal: 32 (bottom left), 39, 86.
Bibliothèque de l'Institut Opthalmologique: 12 (center right).
Bibliothèque de Poitiers: 67.
Bibliothèque des Arts Décoratifs: 1, 2, 3, 12 (top and center left), 26, 32 (bottom right), 86.
Bibliothèque Forney: 26, 29.
Bibliothèque Nationale: 7, 12 (bottom left), 32 (top right).
The Charleston Trust: 179, 180, 181.
Ecomusée de la Grande Lande: 50 (bottom left), 105.
Faringdon Collection Trust: 121.
HG/Condé Nast: 61, 68, 83 (top), 85, 97, 104, 115, 125 (top), 135, 144, 147, 154–55, 161, 175.
Leeds Castle Foundation: 58, 108.
Marie-Claire: 102.
Musée Charles Demery: 30–31, 38.
Musée de la Toile de Jouy: 36–37, 50 (excluding bottom left), 51, 52–53.
Musée de l'Impression sur Etoffes: vi, 28, 40, 46, 47.
Musée des Arts Décoratifs: 158–59.
Musée National de la Voiture et du Tourisme, Compiegne: 151.
National Flax Museum: 8–9, 56.
National Trust, 112, 162.
National Trust/Victoria and Albert Museum: 120 (top), 150.
Marie-Claude Orsoni: 17.
La Passementerie Nouvelle: 132, 133, back jacket (top left).
Prelle Lyon: 18, 66, 76, 77, 78, 79, 80.
Rubelli: 27, 54, 69, 73 (bottom left and right).
Tassinari & Chatel: ii, iii, 25, 82.
Victoria Mansion Museum: 91.
World of Interiors: 50 (bottom left), 105, 176–77.

index